Work Experience Level 5

Arlene Douglas and Séamus O'Neill

g GILL EDUCATION

Gill Education
Hume Avenue
Park West
Dublin 12
www.gilleducation.ie

Gill Education is an imprint of M.H. Gill & Co.

978 07171 59710

Illustrations by Derry Dillon
Print origination by O'K Graphic Design, Dublin
Printed and bound by CPI Group (UK) Ltd, Croydon, CR0 4YY

A CIP catalogue record is available for this book from the British Library.

Contents

Chapter 1	General Work-related Information	1
Chapter 2	Planning and Preparing for Work Experience	20
Chapter 3	Vocational Study	58
Chapter 4	Work and the Law: Basic Rights and Responsibilities of Employees and Employers	74
Chapter 5	The Work Placement	91
Chapter 6	Reflecting on the Work Placement Experience	106
Chapter 7	Future Planning	115
Chapter 8	Skills Demonstration: Supervisor Reports	123
Chapter 9	Work Practice	133
Chapter 10	FETAC/QQI Level 6 Work Experience	140

This book is dedicated to all those who are willing to work hard to secure a job that they will enjoy.

CHAPTER 1

General Work-related Information

Organisational Change in Recent Years

Since 2010, total employment in Ireland has fallen by over 300,000, or almost 15%. Even though the working age population has risen, the labour supply has fallen because some people have withdrawn from the labour market altogether. The unemployment rate has soared from 4.8% to 14.2% in this short period. Some 166,000 jobs disappeared in the construction sector alone – the sector that fuelled the Celtic Tiger from 1997 to 2007. Jobs have also been lost in the accommodation and hospitality sector as well as the services sector and agriculture.

All economic sectors have experienced a massive decline, except for public administration, health and education – over 70% of the employees in those sectors are state employees. However, state employees have experienced a huge decline in wages and salary levels following the Croke Park and Haddington Road Agreements. Stronger export figures were recorded in 2011, and more recently, Irish competitiveness was expected to improve, thus stimulating job creation in export services, tourism and manufacturing.

Types of Work Organisations

The following are the general types (categories) of organisations.

Types of Organisations	Structures and Roles
Sole proprietor	<ul><li>Usually unincorporated (i.e. they do not have company status).</li><li>Owned by one person who receives all the profits but also incurs all the liabilities or debts personally.</li><li>Must register a trade name with the Companies Registration Office (CRO) – Registration of Business Names Act 1963, although this alone does not protect the name from being copied (you must register a trademark to protect a logo or brand name).</li></ul>
Partnership	<ul><li>Tends to be used for professional practices, such as solicitors and accountants, or small and medium-sized enterprises (SMEs) with two to 50 partners.</li><li>Limited partnerships allowing one or more general partners to manage the daily affairs of the business are less common.</li><li>The Partnership Act 1890 ensures profits are shared equally; alternatively, the deed of partnership specifies the agreed profit distribution.</li></ul>

Unincorporated associations	• In an unincorporated association, a group of individuals come together to carry out a mutual activity. • This is the most common structure for small sports clubs, as it is a simple and informal way of establishing an organisation (larger sports clubs are usually registered as companies). • Unincorporated associations do not hold too much property or employ staff. An insurance policy can cover liabilities. • A set of rules are drawn up by trustees, while a committee runs club affairs. • A trust is the classic form under which clubs have operated for many years, governed by a document called a trust deed. • The people in the club who are responsible for its finances are called the trustees. • Trustees will have to be appointed if the organisation wishes to hold property, such as a clubhouse.
Public limited company (plc)	• These are usually large companies with large turnover (sales) quoted on a stock exchange. • Public limited companies place 'plc' after their company name, for example Independent News & Media plc, Ryanair Holdings plc. • For a full listing of public companies, see www.crmz.com/Directory/CountryIE.htm or www.cro.ie.
Private limited company	• These are often SMEs. • They are represented by Irish business representative bodies, namely the Irish Business and Employers Confederation (IBEC), the Small Firms Association (SFA) and the Irish Small and Medium Enterprises Association (ISME). • Retailers are a large section of the tertiary services sector and are represented by Retail Ireland (part of IBEC) and RGDATA for the grocery sector.
Friendly societies	• These are mainly group community schemes, small trade unions, some clubs and societies. Agricultural co-operatives were traditionally registered as friendly societies. • They must be registered under the Registrar of Friendly Societies (see www.cro.ie).
Credit unions	• Credit unions are registered under the Registrar of Credit Unions (see www.centralbank.ie).

State bodies and public sector organisations (government organisations)	• Organisations that are totally funded by the government, such as nurses, teachers, police and civil servants working in government agencies. • Some are trading (take in money from the public) and some are non-trading organisations. For example, the army is a non-trading state body, whereas public hospitals are a trading state body.
Semi-state bodies	• Organisations that are partly funded by the government (public sector) and partly by the private sector, such as CIÉ or ESB. • Some are trading (take in money from the public) and some are non-trading bodies. For example, a transportation organisation such as Bus Éireann or Irish Rail is a trading semi-state body, whereas the Industrial Development Authority (IDA) and Shannon Development are non-trading semi-state bodies.
Charities (voluntary sector)	• Charities have historically been run as unincorporated associations. • A trust is the classic form under which charities have operated for many years and is a type of unincorporated association governed by a document called a trust deed. • The people who run the charity and are responsible for its finances are called the trustees.
Caring groups (voluntary sector)	• This includes groups that give advice, such as the Samaritans, Cura or Childline.

Which category does the organisation where you intend doing your work experience fit into?

Organisations for the Future

According to Solas (formerly FÁS), there are reasonable job prospects in the following areas as the country emerges from recession:
• **Jobs with high turnover**, such as shop assistants, clerical workers, childcare, care of the elderly, catering, hairdressing and security.
• **Growth areas** include sales of second-hand goods, repair and maintenance, bookies, fast food, door-to-door selling and green energy.

- **Long-term demand occupations** include engineering, computing, science and medical, legal and financial services.

Where can jobs be found in Ireland? The following is a flavour of where jobs might be available in the future.

The Games Sector

A report entitled *The Games Sector in Ireland – An Action Plan for Growth* (October 2011), which was carried out by Forfás, said that action needed to be taken to position Ireland as one of the most progressive and digitally advanced business environments.

Organisations need to change their strategies and develop business where demand is proven to exist. We all know about gadgets and interactive games; a global demand clearly appears to exist in this sector. According to Martin Shanahan, chief executive of Forfás, 'Games can also be a catalyst for growth in a host of other related activities in the digital economy, including social networks, search engines, animation, film and video and e-learning.' New organisations might base their future business plans on sectors such as games, film and animation. Direct job creation as well as spin-off jobs could result from such developments.

The Environment and Green Technologies Sector

According to the 2011 Environmental Protection Agency (EPA) support guide for businesses, *Developing a Green Enterprise*, 'companies are becoming increasingly aware of the financial savings and competitive advantages that arise from adopting an environmentally sustainable and resource-efficient approach to their business. The increasing demand from consumers and clients for "green" and sustainable products and services also provides new opportunities for enterprises to meet customer needs.'

Gaps in Organisations

Skills shortages exist in professions such as doctors, nurses, software engineers, accountants with expertise in regulation, technical sales representatives and IT specialists. Growth areas include the food industry and exporting, pharmaceuticals, and media and communications.

According to the *National Skills Bulletin 2011* compiled for FÁS by the Expert Group on Future Skills Needs, 'skills shortages were identified in a survey conducted by the FÁS (SLMRU) Recruitment Agency Survey (*National Skills Bulletin 2011*) indicating that positions were difficult to fill in the digital content and technology sector, in sectors like engineering and utilities (e.g. metal working, production and maintenance fitters, electrical engineers, motor mechanics), and ICT (e.g. computer installation and maintenance), in high-technology activities like pharmaceutical activities, medical devices, managerial, senior posts and sales positions. It also listed high-level niche areas like accountants, tax experts, actuaries, business analysts, statisticians, planners, medical practitioners and chemists as occupations that are difficult to fill.'

Where will the best-paying jobs be in Ireland 2015?

What career paths should the classes of 2012 follow in order to make a living after college? If the school leavers don't know by now, they'd better make up something quickly, because it's CAO form-filling time.

Yes, the deadline to decide what you want to do with the rest of your life comes up at the end of January. So no pressure then, eh?

Traditionally safe and lucrative professions are looking dicey: banking, teaching, medicine, architecture – they're not the solid ways to earn a livelihood that they once were.

So, where will the jobs be when you graduate in 2015, and what courses can you choose in order to bag them?

Technology and science

No surprises here. Forty per cent of new jobs in coming years will be in the technology and science arena, the IDA has predicted.

Companies like Zynga, Quest, Google, Intel and Amgen have made big investments here in the past 12 months, and that bodes well for employment prospects in a few years' time.

The IDA has €600m-plus worth of business wins lined up for 2012, mainly in the technology, biotechnology and science fields.

'The technology sector generated 4,000 jobs last year,' said ICT Ireland director Paul Sweetman, 'and there will be 200 job announcements this month alone.'

So courses like software engineering, computer science, software development and design are ones to consider.

Meanwhile, big pharma should continue to be a big employer. Billion-dollar drug maker Alkermes came to Ireland in 2011, and Botox maker Allergan announced a €270m expansion in Westport, happening over the next four years and adding 200 jobs there.

Earning power: €40,000 a year and upwards

Gambling

Not putting your college money on a horse, but rather considering the bookmaking sector as a great career bet. The growth of online gambling is opening up huge opportunities here.

'The business needs maths graduates, actuarial graduates, computer programmers, digital marketers, social media and Google analytics experts,' said Sharon Byrne of the Irish Bookmakers' Association.

Now Europe's biggest bookmaker, Paddy Power, employs 2,500 people. Its graduate trainee programme takes on people with degrees in business, IT, e-commerce, maths, statistics, marketing and business analytics.

Earning power: Paddy Power grads get an 'attractive package' including salary, bonus, pension, healthcare and life cover

Accountancy

It's one of the few traditional safe havens left. Big four firms KPMG, PwC, Ernst & Young and Deloitte have been taking in more graduates despite the economic gloom. There's big money to be made in handling all these administrations, receiverships, liquidations and restructurings that the recession has brought about.

You don't need to have an accountancy degree; a good 2:1 degree in any discipline could get you in.

Earning power: Starting at around €20,000 a year for graduate trainees, with potential to move into six figures if you're made partner in a big firm

Lidl/Aldi manager

Retail spend may be falling off a cliff but people still need to eat. The two German discounters have been eating up market share and opening new branches monthly.

Both Lidl and Aldi have rather well-paid graduate programmes. You need a decent 2:1 degree in any discipline to apply.

Lidl funds its own retail management degree in partnership with the Dublin Business School and even pays students a salary and holiday leave throughout their studies. (Application is via Lidl directly rather than the CAO system.)

Earning power: A €60,000 starting salary plus a fully expensed car. At Aldi the car is an Audi A4 – not bad at all if you're 22 and fresh out of college. Salary rises to more than €80,000 over time.

IFSC back office

It's cold comfort to Ulster Bank employees, but if financial services tsar John Bruton follows through on his mission, the IFSC will employ thousands more in coming years. This is where back office and clearing house functions are carried out for some of the biggest companies in the world: hedge funds, reinsurance giants, banks and asset financing firms.

On top of the 33,000 people employed there, there's a plan to provide 10,000 more jobs there over the next five years. Almost 90% of employees there are third-level graduates.

Earning power: €50,000-plus

Agrifood

Companies like Glanbia and Kerry Group are turning a tasty profit despite the recession and the agrifood sector is the second biggest employer in the country.

Points for degree courses in fields like agribusiness and food innovation leapt up by an average of more than 20 points last year.

Kerry Group recruits graduate trainees from disciplines as diverse as finance, engineering, IT, product development and science. Glanbia looks for food technologists, business analysts, finance, IT, engineering and food science graduates.

Earning power: Circa €20,000 during graduate traineeship, then €50,000-plus

Aviation finance

Almost all of the world's big aircraft leasing firms have offices in Ireland and it's a multi-billion-euro industry.

Aviation leasing hires a big mix of professions, as it takes a cross-section of people to put complex deals together, including lawyers, accountants, sales people, credit risk analysts, engineers and marketers. Training tends to be in-house and informal.

'While Europe is very shut down in the current market, business is booming in Asia and Latin America,' one aviation leasing executive said.

Earning power: Six figures plus bonus, once your career is in full flight

Fast food

The company that runs KFC and Pizza Hut in Ireland made big profits last year, and Supermac's and McDonald's are growing their businesses. McD's is planning an €8m-a-year expansion for the next four to five years. While it doesn't have a dedicated programme, graduates who enlist at management level make a decent living.

Earning power: A second assistant manager at McDonald's makes around €38,000 plus benefits like healthcare. A business manager makes up to €59,000.

Entrepreneurship

Your parents won't thank us for telling you this, but skipping college altogether can be profitable too. Steve Jobs was a college dropout, and that didn't exactly hold the Apple founder back.

The Irish entrepreneur behind one of last year's biggest deals left school early. Greg Turley sold part of his business, Cartrawler, for a cool €100m.

Michelle Mone, the Scottish businesswoman who founded the Ultimo bra empire, left school at 15. Her company is worth €20m.

Earning power: Extremely variable, but potentially huge

Source: Irish Independent

JOB NEWS

Food industry and exporting: According to Bord Bia, food and drink exports were up 8.6% in the first half of 2013.

Pharmaceutical: US-based pharmaceutical Alexion is to create 50 pharmaceutical jobs in Dublin. IDA Ireland, which is backing the new jobs, said Alexion's arrival in Ireland means that seven of the world's top 10 bio-pharma companies now operate in the country.

Media and communications:
- BSkyB has reported a 6% rise in pre-tax profits, with the broadcasting firm making £1.26 billion in the year to the end of June.
- BT Ireland has seen its revenue increase by 2%, according to the company's latest quarterly results.
- Facebook, the world's biggest social network, made $333 million in net income from April to June compared with a net loss of $157 million a year ago, according to the company's latest financial results.

Source: RTÉ News

Career Opportunities

Now you need to examine possible work or career opportunities that would suit you. For example, you could start by identifying relevant needs or gaps in organisations where your skills might meet the needs of the organisation.

CHAPTER EXERCISE: ORGANISATION ANALYSIS

Fill in the table below with the following information:
- List five organisations that might need you based on the skills you have or hope to have soon.
- For each organisation, list the skills you have that this organisation might need and why.
- List the work hours, dress code, pay and challenges you would expect to encounter as well as what this job could lead to in terms of career progression.

Name of organisation	My Relevant Skills	Work Hours	Dress Code	Pay	Challenges	Career Progression
1.						
2.						
3.						
4.						
5.						

The information that I have put into the above table is based on an online job search I carried out on [date] . . . .

My Career Plan – Where Will I Be in 10 Years?

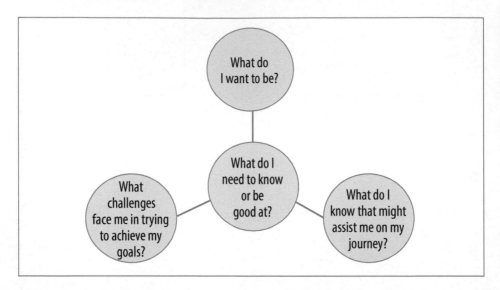

Carry out a quick SWOT analysis (strengths, weaknesses, opportunities, threats) of yourself.

My Strengths	My Weaknesses	My Opportunities	My Threats

Goals	Action Points
My goals for work experience and beyond	How I propose to get where I am going

Work-related Issues, Trends and Needs

Why is it important to learn about workplace issues or problems? Because you might face some of these issues in the workplace and you will need to know how to deal with them or how to solve them.

The following are common work-related issues.

- **Health and safety:** There might be workplace hazards that could be dangerous or cause an accident. The Health and Safety Authority (HSA) promotes health and safety at work and provides information on a wide variety of work-related topics to employers and employees. Visit the HSA website (www.hsa.ie) for valuable current advice based on the Safety, Health and Welfare at Work Act 2005.
- **Discrimination:** Discrimination happens when one person or group of people are treated unfairly or differently to others. There are nine grounds of discrimination, including gender and race.
- **Harassment and threatening or offensive behaviour:** This could be verbal, physical or sexual.
- **Respecting co-workers:** Respect is a fundamental requirement for good working relationships between workers.
- **Managing employees:** Punctuality (late arriving), attire for work (how you dress), absenteeism (frequently out without a good reason), lack of initiative (slow to act).
- **Using social media while at work:** Almost half of Irish employers don't have a social media policy in place, which leaves them open to problems or abuse.
- **Job stress and work–life balance:** Stress is a reason for absenteeism in the workplace. A balance must be reached to allow workers to experience job satisfaction and to stay healthy too.

What Work or Career Opportunities Will Suit You?

Having explored where jobs might be available in the future, you now need to pinpoint possible personal work or career opportunities that will suit you. Identify relevant needs or gaps in organisations.

- Identify your personal skill sets that match specific areas of employment.
- Consider the work-related issues that a job will entail:
    - ◆ Work hours: See Chapter 4 for work hour limits.
    - ◆ Pay: See Chapter 4 for minimum wage rates.
    - ◆ Health and safety: See Chapter 4 for safety requirements for workers.

- ◆ Employee rights, legislation and work-related challenges: See Chapter 4 for information on employee rights, employment legislation and work-related challenges, including positive action, diversity and equality.
- ◆ Attire for work: See Chapter 2 for information on attire, appearance and dress.
- ◆ Career progression: Log on to the FETAC/QQI websites (www.fetac. ie or www.qqi.ie) or CAO website (www.cao.ie) for information about further education and higher education courses respectively.

Identify the skill sets you will need and review the section on the challenges you may encounter in your area (see Exercise on p. 11). Use a highlighter to identify what you are good at and where your interests lie, as listed in the table below.

What am I good at or interested in?	What could I do?	Opportunities	Search for possible jobs that you are interested in (list the website address in this column)
Media studies, journalism, English, creative writing, communications	Journalist Writer or novelist Radio or TV presenter or producer (broadcast journalism courses, social media courses – day and short night courses)	Work for RTÉ, TG4, TV3, local media (check www. medialive.ie for a full media contacts listing)	

Languages, sign language, communications	Call centre operator (business course is an advantage)	Work for the IFSC Work in a call centre www.siliconrepublic.com	
	Sign language teacher	National Learning Network www.irishdeafyouth.com www.deafhear.ie	
	Translator	Work for the IFSC, in teleservices or call centres	
Sports and leisure, recreation studies	Leisure centre assistant	Work in a leisure centre	
	Coach	Set up your own business, e.g. running an athletics club	
	Referee	Work for the GAA, FAI or IRFU	
Mathematics, IT	Accountant, bookkeeper, payroll	Work for an accountancy organisation	
	Statistician	Work for the Central Statistics Office (CSO)	
	Computer programmer	Work for many different organisations	
Social studies	International aid worker/ NGO	Work for Goal, Trócaire, St Vincent de Paul, Department of Foreign Affairs and Trade, Irish Aid	
	Social worker (courses in social studies, youth and community work, and community development)	Work for the HSE, Department of Health and Children	

Agriculture, horticulture	Food specialist	Work for food companies to test products	
	Farming, horticulture	Work in a garden centre or set up your own	
	Florist (night and day courses in garden design, floristry)	Work in a flower shop or set up your own	
Science, biology, medicine	Environmental scientist	Work for the Environmental Protection Agency (EPA)	
	Scientist	Work as an earth and ocean scientist	
	Nutritionist	Work in a hospital advising patients on nutrition	
	Laboratory technician	Work as a lab technician	
	Pharmacy assistant	Work in pharmaceuticals	
	Doctor, nurse	Work in a hospital	
	Vet or veterinary assistant	Work in the zoo or a veterinary clinic	

Geography	Meteorologist	Work for Met Éireann	
	Weather presenter (need broadcasting course)	Work for RTÉ or TV3	
	Teacher of geography or tourism	Work as a teacher in a school or for Fáilte Ireland	
	Tour operator	Set up your own business, e.g. as a tour guide	
	Archaeologist	Work for the Department of the Environment	
Administration, information and communications technology (ICT)	Computer programmer	Work for many different organisations	
	Administrator	Work for any organisation in a front office capacity	
	HR/personnel manager	Work for any organisation in the HR department	
Childcare, community care	Childminder	Work in a crèche	
	Special needs assistant	Work in a primary school	
	Carer of older persons	Work in a nursing home	
	Primary school teacher (need honours Irish and to be good with children)	Work in a primary school	
	Secondary school teacher	Work in a secondary school	
Engineering	Civil engineer	Work as a civil engineer	
	Mechanical engineer	Work as a mechanical engineer	

Interior design, architecture	Interior designer	Work for a builder, developer or private clients	
	Architect	Work for an architecture firm, developer or set up your own business	
Multimedia, IT, graphics	Web designer (multimedia)	Set up your own website design business	
Art, craft, design	Artist (painting, drawing, mosaic specialist courses)	Set up your own gallery	
	Fashion designer (dressmaking, knitwear)	Work for clothing companies or yourself	
	Ceramics or glass specialist	Work for Tipperary Crystal, Newbridge Cutlery	
	Jeweller	Set up your own business	
	Upholsterer	Set up your own business	
Arts: Visual drama, music, dance, sound engineering	Music or dance teacher, musician, composer, singer	Work for yourself giving music lessons or dance lessons, be a singer-songwriter	
Construction	Builder	Work in construction	
	Carpenter	Set up your own business	
Hair and beauty	Hairdresser	Work in a salon or set up your own business	
	Beautician	Work in a spa or set up your own business	
Hotel, catering, tourism	Chef Hotel manager (need course in management) Travel agent (mostly online businesses now)	Work in a hotel or restaurant	

Religious education	Priest	Do voluntary work	
	Nun	Work in the community	
	Missionary	Work abroad as a missionary	
Accounting, banking, insurance	Accountant	Work in partnership or set up your own business	
	Banker	Work in a financial institution, bank, building society	
	Insurance broker	Set up your own business	
	Auctioneer	Set up your own business	

CHAPTER EXERCISE CHECKLIST

Make sure you have included all the exercises in this chapter in your learner's portfolio.

Chapter Exercise	Completed
Analyse five organisations that might need you based on the skills you have or hope to have soon	

What Needs to Be in the Learner's Portfolio?

Planning and Preparation Section
- An exploration of work organisations
- An exploration of personal career opportunities in a particular vocational area, to include consideration of work-related issues, trends and needs

CHAPTER 2

Planning and Preparing for Work Experience

"OK, first things first. Can I see your permit?"

LEARNING OUTCOMES:

- PRODUCE A SKILLS AUDIT.
- EXAMINE WORKPLACE INTERACTIONS.
- ESTABLISH WORK EXPERIENCE GOALS.
- IDENTIFY EDUCATION AND TRAINING NEEDS.
- DETERMINE VARIOUS JOB-FINDING STRATEGIES.
- PREPARE FOR AN INTERVIEW.

The saying 'if you fail to prepare, prepare to fail' is apt when starting a work experience programme. You need to spend some time planning and preparing before going on work experience. This planning and preparation process must then be clearly documented under appropriate headings.

Personal and workplace details:
- Name
- Award title and code
- Course title
- Course definition – a brief summary of the course
- Subjects being studied
- Proposed career path
- Desired location of future work
- Work experience day(s)
- Proposed times allocated to work experience

Skills Audit

A skills audit involves identifying the skills that you have learned already and where you learned them. You may have acquired many of these skills at home, in school or through previous work situations. These should be easily identified.

Personal Skills

Personal skills are individual skills and are linked to personality traits, such as the ability to work on your own initiative, meet deadlines, complete tasks successfully, be punctual, speak clearly and be able to work under pressure.

Personal Skills	Examples
I'm punctual and have a good attendance record.	I worked in industry for three years and was never late for work. I have very few sick days on record.
I'm reliable and able to work on my own initiative.	When employed, I was able to take instruction and work on my own – I can supply references to prove it.
I'm adaptable/flexible.	Even though I only worked part time, when retraining was required in the company I worked at, I was willing to retrain in order to become computer literate and I adapted very well to the new work practices.
I'm efficient, committed and good at completing tasks efficiently and meeting deadlines.	When we were organising the school graduation I was allocated the task of jointly producing a graduation booklet. We produced this to meet a set deadline for the printers.

I'm a confident person and will dress in a smart, appropriate fashion/I will be conscious of company image.	I have worked part time as an office administrator and in sales and always dress smartly, usually in a sharp white shirt (and tie) and suit when appropriate, with minimal jewellery and make-up, paying attention to hygiene at all times. This helped me with self-confidence. I've been taught that where customers are concerned, first impressions are lasting.
I'm trustworthy, patient and even-tempered.	My previous workplace will verify that I handled complaints and awkward customers very well and remained patient at all times.
I'm good-humoured and have a positive, proactive approach to my work.	My school and my previous workplace will verify that I get on well with classmates, teachers, colleagues and managers and like to move along with my work instead of wasting time. I like to make suggestions for improvements to the workplace when it is appropriate to do so. I also have a good social life.
I'm discreet, respectful and reliable.	I babysat for a couple for a significant amount of time and respected their privacy at all times.
I'm aware of when and when not to articulate my opinion.	I like to make suggestions for improvements to the workplace when it is appropriate to do so and realise that it is not always appropriate to voice your opinion.
I'm conscious of maintaining confidentiality and proper company ethics.	I have never discussed information of a personal nature with colleagues or managers to prevent rumours, which are unprofessional and bad for workplace relations and reputation.
I'm able to take responsibility and have leadership skills.	I like to take the lead when it comes to organising and making decisions. I captained my local football team, as the manager will verify.
I'm a good organiser.	I compiled rosters for my local youth club.

Interpersonal Skills

Interpersonal skills are often referred to as 'soft' or 'people' skills, such as the ability to deal with people effectively and efficiently and work as part of a team. These skills are displayed when a learner has good communication skills.

Interpersonal Skills	Examples
I communicate well with *employers/ managers* and respect authority.	I have had successful dealings with former teachers and the manager of the local hurling club that I play for.
I communicate well with *colleagues* and *work partners*.	While in school I was part of a team that organised various sixth year events and our graduation night.
I enjoy working with *customers/ clients*.	I work part time in the local corner shop.
I enjoy contacting and transacting with *suppliers*.	I worked for my father, who owns a glass shop display business. He set me the task of pricing materials for use in his business.
I have experience dealing with *staff who work in personnel and human resources*.	I worked in an HR office for the summer and helped to design a number of advertisements for job vacancies that existed. I had to agree with the manager and change a number of details until we got the ad right.
I have experience in negotiating.	I worked for a students' union and dealt with grievances and problems that some students had to the best of my ability.
I have good speaking skills/ telephone techniques.	I worked as an office administrator and answered the phone efficiently and courteously.
I am aware of my body language when dealing with customers and always try to be confident and helpful.	I had to deal with awkward and rude customers and I did this in a calm and reassuring way, always prioritising the customer.
I will always follow up and give appropriate feedback when dealing with customers.	In my capacity as office administrator, I had to call customers back when a consignment of goods that they had ordered arrived. Good customer service skills were also needed to deal with a number of complaints and I followed up by phoning the customers and apologising for any inconvenience.

Dealing with Customers

When dealing with customers, there are two types of professional interaction:

- Face-to-face interaction
- Telephone techniques

The following questions will help you identify what kind of face-to-face interpersonal skills you possess.

* Are you good with people?
* Do you have a likeable personality?
* Are you a good listener?
* Are you a respectful person?
* Are you tactful?
* Are you obliging?
* Do you always put the customer first?
* If possible, would you offer the customer a cup of tea or coffee while they were waiting to see a manager?
* Is it true that you never argue with a customer and that you always apologise for any inconvenience, even if you know the customer was at fault?
* How do you answer the phone in a work situation?
* Have you adopted a professional telephone manner?
* Do you use the correct greeting based on the time of day?
* Do you state your name and offer your assistance?
* If you have to put the caller on hold, do you ask if they mind holding and wait for their answer?
* Do you always check with your superior or colleague to see if he or she is free to take the call?
* Do you always adopt a professional approach and obtain the caller's name before you put the call through to a superior or colleague?

ROLE PLAY

Telephonist: Good afternoon, Smyth and Cox Brothers Ltd. My name is Mary, how may I help you?

Caller: I wish to speak to John Smyth, please.

Telephonist: Certainly, sir. Can I say who is calling, please?

Caller: My name is James Turner.

Telephonist: Thank you, Mr Turner. Would you mind if I put you on hold for a moment while I see if Mr Smyth is in his office?

Caller: That's fine.

Telephonist: All right, just hold for a moment, thank you.

- Do you always quickly return to the caller and never leave them on hold for more than a few seconds?
- Do you always take the caller's name and telephone number if necessary and ask if they want you to note what the call was regarding?
- Do you always get the message immediately to the person that it is intended for?

Dealing with Work Colleagues or Partners

Along with the qualities already outlined above, the following are desirable when dealing with work colleagues.
- Be a good communicator (speaking and listening).
- Work effectively and efficiently as part of a team.
- Be supportive of colleagues.
- Are you even-tempered?
- Do you always make an effort to get on well with work colleagues generally?
- Would you oblige a colleague by covering work hours when they cannot work?

Dealing with Suppliers

When dealing with suppliers, it is important to realise that there are two different types of purchase.
- Cash purchase, i.e. cash paid over the counter.
- Credit purchase, i.e. purchases on account where it has been agreed that the business has 30 or 60 days' credit. In other words, the business does not have to pay the bill until a month or two after it is received.

When ordering from suppliers, it is important to take the initiative and shop around to get the best value for money.

If you have dealings with suppliers while on work experience, be sure to:
- Check what the business supplies.
- Know what is being ordered and get written confirmation of the order as well as the time, date and nature of the order. (Most businesses have their own order forms that can be e-mailed to the supplier.)
- Be firm but courteous with suppliers and always check with your supervisor if you are unsure of anything.

- Have you priced around to get the best value for money?
- Do you know what this supplier provides and how long the business has been ordering goods or services from them?
- Do you know the terms of trade and if any discounts are allowed? (This can usually be found on quotations received.)
- Did you check with your supervisor before you phoned the supplier to clarify details?

Dealing with the Employer or Manager

When dealing with managers, an employee must:
- Portray a bright, cheery and positive image.
- Be trustworthy.
- Be confident regarding your abilities.
- Work on your own initiative.
- Be adaptable.
- Be flexible regarding work hours.
- Be committed.
- Carry out instructions efficiently.
- Accept constructive criticism about your appearance, punctuality and general work conduct,
- Report back to management effectively and efficiently.
- Be even-tempered.
- Never criticise your employer or superior unless it is constructive criticism and is non-confrontational.
- Act on suggestions for personal improvements.

Dealing with HR or Personnel Departments

If you are required to deal with an HR head office, make sure you do the following.
- Check with your supervisor if you are dealing with personal details connected with a staff member.
- Know what staff you are enquiring about and their exact status.
- Brief yourself on who exactly you are to speak with in the HR department.

- Always maintain confidentiality when handling personal information – be aware of the Data Protection Act and the rights of employees as well as employer obligations (see Chapter 4).

Vocational Skills

Vocational, or 'hard', skills are those that are required to do a specific job or to work in a particular trade.

Some people develop vocational skills in school or college and/or apprenticeship programmes. Examples of different vocational skill sets are those required to work as a:
- Beautician
- Car mechanic
- Chef
- Computer technician
- Hairdresser
- Photographer
- Website developer

Vocational Skills	Examples
Design a company leaflet using Microsoft Publisher.	I have references from the print company that I worked for and samples of my work in a portfolio.
Design interiors, having studied on a one-year interior design course.	I have a certificate in interior design and worked part time for a home interiors designer. Written and verbal references are available.
I can compile and use spreadsheets.	I have a certificate to show competence in Microsoft Excel.
I can use modern sewing machines and make clothes and curtains.	I worked in a curtain shop part time for over two years and have references and work samples available.
I have very good writing skills and have some radio broadcasting skills.	I had articles published in a number of different media publications (samples available) and worked part time for a local radio station.
I was a plumber and did a three-year apprenticeship.	I have references and a trade certificate.

More examples of a range of vocational skills that can be learned in different vocational areas are outlined in the following table.

Computers and business	Produce a letter in a word processing program Set up a working database of clients Develop a company website Calculate wages, VAT, etc. Produce a cash flow analysis on a spreadsheet
Beauty care	Aromatherapy Electrolysis Eyebrow shaping and trimming Facials Make-up Reflexology Waxing
Art and design	Design solutions from a given design brief Use pre-press and press techniques Geometrical constructions Use colour separation techniques
Floristry	Cutting Arrange dried flowers Make hand-tied bouquets Advise customers when taking orders Water and tidy plants Make buttonholes Green a wreath
Retail	Advertising Cash and stock control Computerised space planning Costing Pricing Receiving orders and estimating margins Signage Visual merchandising shop display

The Importance of Interests and Hobbies

Employers will judge job applicants on qualifications, experience and skills. However, a person's skills will often be easy to identify through their interests and hobbies.

Interest or Hobby	What It Shows
I captained my local hurling team.	Leadership skills
I love animals. I do pony trekking twice a week and clean the animals.	Hard worker and a caring person
I enjoy playing piano and guitar in my spare time.	Musical and creative attributes
I like to make my own clothes.	A stylish and creative person with new ideas
I fly small aircraft and own a few vintage cars.	A risk taker/image conscious
I play football for my home team.	Works well as part of a team
I do kickboxing.	Enjoys a challenge, defensive abilities
I enjoy gardening and learning about new plants and garden design.	Creative and interested in the outdoors
I buy art and invest in stocks and shares.	A creative risk taker with good business acumen

Skills Checklist

In the following exercises, you are required to compile a personal, interpersonal and vocational skills checklist identifying your:
- Strengths
- Talents
- Personal qualities and attributes
- Interests
- Practical skills appropriate to the vocational area (your chosen work area)
- Prior learning

CHAPTER EXERCISE: YOUR SKILLS

Complete the following skills checklist by listing your personal, interpersonal and vocational skills and then rating them.

	EXCELLENT	VERY GOOD	GOOD	FAIR	POOR
PERSONAL SKILLS					
INTERPERSONAL SKILLS					
VOCATIONAL SKILLS					

CHAPTER EXERCISE: YOUR TALENTS OR STRENGTHS

From the list of personal skills you gave in Exercise 1, choose your three top talents or strengths. Enter the details in the table below.

TALENTS OR STRENGTHS	
1.	
2.	
3.	

CHAPTER EXERCISE: YOUR INTERESTS OR HOBBIES

List your top five interests and/or hobbies in the table below.

INTERESTS AND/OR HOBBIES	
1.	
2.	
3.	
4.	
5.	

CHAPTER EXERCISE: YOUR PRACTICAL/VOCATIONAL SKILLS

In the table below, list five practical ('hard') skills that you possess that you believe are relevant to your chosen career. Specify where you learned these skills.

PRACTICAL/VOCATIONAL SKILLS		
	Skill	**Where I Learned It**
1.		
2.		
3.		
4.		
5.		

CHAPTER EXERCISE: WHY I AM AN ASSET TO THE ORGANISATION

Explain how the personal, interpersonal and vocational skills that you have identified would be an asset to the organisation that you are applying to for work experience.

_____

_____

_____

_____

_____

_____

Goals for Work Experience

What Is a Career Plan?

A career plan is like a road map that guides you to your chosen job or occupation. A good career plan will include the learning goals necessary for you to achieve in order to acquire the skills and knowledge to do a particular job.

What Is a Goal?

A goal is a target you set or an objective you work towards and aim to achieve. Learners are encouraged to set clear and unambiguous goals for their work experience and document them.

Career goals can be classified into short, medium or long term, which will lead a person to their chosen job. Examples of new career skills you may hope to achieve as a result of goals set while on work experience are categorised as follows.

1. Long-term goals: The knowledge and skills required to achieve these goals are more likely to be built up over a number of years.
- Deal confidently with customers.
- Act astutely when dealing with different personality types.
- Graduate with a third-level degree.

2. Medium-term goals: The knowledge and skills required to achieve these goals are more likely to be learned over a number of months.
- Cut and colour hair.
- Design and develop a company website.
- Shoot and edit footage for a promotional DVD or YouTube upload.
- Teach young children how to swim at a local swimming academy.
- Learn how to use social networking media such as Facebook or Twitter to promote a business.
- Produce a range of pastry desserts for a special occasion, such as a wedding reception.

3. Short-term goals: The knowledge and skills required to achieve these goals are more likely to be mastered over a number of hours or days.

- Type a memo.
- Design a shop window display.
- Carry out a hot stone back massage.
- Secure a computer against spyware and viruses.
- Manage a hotel booking for a party of German anglers.
- Produce a detailed costing of a self-catering sun holiday to one of the Balearic Islands for a family of four.

What Are Action Points?

Action points are the specific activities that you carry out in order to achieve your goal(s).

For example, if your goal is to produce a website for the company or organisation where you are doing your work experience, then you will need to set out the action points necessary to achieve this goal. For example:

- Talk to the manager about the requirements for the website.
- Gain website design and page layout skills.
- Learn how to use a website design program, such as Adobe Dreamweaver.
- Obtain a web address (URL) for the company.
- Engage the services of a website hosting company.
- Produce the website.
- Upload and test the website.

CHAPTER EXERCISE: YOUR GOALS

Now set and list your short-, medium- and long-term goals and respective action points for your work experience.

	Short-term Goals	Action Points
1.		
2.		

3.		
4.		

	Medium-term Goals	Action Points
1.		
2.		
3.		
4.		

	Long-term Goals	Action Points
1.		
2.		

3.		
4.		

Challenges to Achieving Goals

Career and work experience goals can sometimes be difficult to achieve for a variety of reasons.

* **Incorrect aptitude:** Perhaps the chosen career doesn't suit your aptitude.
* **Poor attitude:** A positive attitude tinged with a little humility are essential.
* **Lack of perseverance:** You might lack the 'staying power' to see a goal achieved.
* **Poor planning:** The action points laid down to achieve a goal are incomplete or badly thought out.
* **Distractions:** You are not focused on achieving the goal in hand.
* **Workplace disharmony:** A workplace can sometimes be an unhappy environment for a number of reasons, such as poor management practices, disgruntled employees, lack of work task variety or bullying.

Education and Training Needs

You must be totally clear as to the educational and training needs of the job to gain employment in your chosen career. For example, a computer technician will need a qualification like the FETAC/QQI Level 5 Computer and Network Maintenance certificate. Ideally, he or she will also require a year's work experience in shadowing an experienced computer technician in the field.

Documents to Prepare for Work Experience

There is nothing worse than badly constructed letters and CVs. When applying for work experience, pay close attention to detail. These documents must be free of spelling and grammatical mistakes. CVs and letters of application must be well laid out and easy to read. Remember: first written impressions are lasting!

If you can't do it yourself, pay a professional to do it for you. Don't exclude information that might be critical to a particular job. It is common for applicants to have slightly different CVs that suit different job positions. For example, when applying for a particular position you might include more details or edit out some details that are not relevant. The following are guidelines to help you compile a clear, concise CV and letter of application for work experience.

Curriculum Vitae (CV)

A CV is a summary of your personal details, qualifications, educational details, work experience, skills and interests/hobbies. It should start at the present and work back into the past. It should be no longer than two A4 pages. In order to make it easy to compile, organise a simple table using a word processing program (e.g. Microsoft Word). Set up two columns and one row. Insert the headings first in size 12 font, upper case and bold. Subheadings, like dates, should be in sentence case (first word only capitalised). The heading Curriculum Vitae should be outside the table and should be typed in upper case, bold and centred. See the sample on the next page.

Sample CV headings are:
- Personal details
- Educational details
- Work experience
- Skills profile
- Interests and hobbies
- Referees

Sample CV

CURRICULUM VITAE	
PERSONAL DETAILS	
Name:	Sarah Moran
Address:	45 Farnham Street
	Cavan
	Co. Cavan
Telephone number:	085-123-6789
EDUCATIONAL DETAILS	
September 2014 to present	Cavan Institute
	Cathedral Road
	Cavan
FETAC/QQI Certificate	**Computer and Network Maintenance**
Course content	Hardware Essentials, Systems Software, Networking Essentials, Computer Programming, Web Authoring, Electronics, Communications and Work Experience
September 2008–June 2014	Loreto College
	Drumkeen
	Cavan
	Co. Cavan
Higher Level	Leaving Certificate
	Maths (D3), French (C3), Business (C2), Biology (D1), Physics (C3)
Lower Level	English (B1), Irish (B3)

WORK EXPERIENCE	
September 2014–present	Retail assistant ByteIT Butlersbridge Co. Cavan
July 2014–present (weekends)	Waitress Cucina's Italian Restaurant Bridge Street Cavan Co. Cavan
SKILLS PROFILE	
Computer literacy	Good working knowledge of Microsoft Windows and Office.
Personal skills	Good people skills and good timekeeper. Experience with dealing with customers in a retail environment.
Achievements	Full, clean driving licence, Grade 8 in Piano Royal Academy of Music. Won various GAA medals in camogie for Loreto College and my club, Cavan Gaels.
Interests	I enjoy playing piano, singing, reading and GAA. I am a member of the Cavan Musical Society.

REFEREES	Mr Joe English, course tutor
	Cavan Institute
	Cathedral Road
	Cavan
	Tel. 049-434-5677
	Ms Lanyi Findelli, proprietor
	Cucina's Italian Restaurant
	Bridge Street
	Cavan
	Co. Cavan
	Tel. 049-434-1234

CHAPTER EXERCISE: YOUR CV

Create a rough draft of your CV (no longer than two pages). Use the headings and template below to help you.

CURRICULUM VITAE	
PERSONAL DETAILS	
EDUCATIONAL DETAILS	

WORK EXPERIENCE	
SKILLS PROFILE	

REFEREES	

Letter of Application for Work Experience

Modern-day letter writing consists of a more straight-line layout, with all information left aligned. The layout is clear, concise and easy to read.

- The second name and address is the name or status of the person you are writing to, e.g. Ms Mary Cotter or The Manager.
- The salutation can either be:
  - ◆ 'Dear Sir or Madam', where the complementary close is 'Yours faithfully' or 'Yours truly'.
  - ◆ 'Dear Ms Cotter', where the complementary close is 'Yours sincerely'.
- The subject heading is the subject of the letter, e.g. Work Experience Application or Job Application.

Sample Letter of Application

22 The Crescent
South Circular Road
Limerick
Co. Limerick

2 October 2015

Ms Kate Mangan
HR Manager
KM Capital Ltd
Shannon
Co. Clare

Dear Ms Mangan,

APPLICATION FOR WORK EXPERIENCE

I wish to apply for work experience with your organisation for the duration of 10 working days, from 8 February 2016 to 19 February 2016 inclusive.

At present I am studying at Limerick College of Further Education and my chosen course of study is a one-year FETAC/QQI Certificate in Marketing with a Language. Work experience is a mandatory module on this course.

I would be very grateful if you could arrange some work experience for me in the area of sales and marketing or customer service.

Please find enclosed a recent edition of my curriculum vitae.

I look forward to hearing from you.

Yours sincerely,

Aisling O'Connor

Aisling O'Connor
Enc.

CHAPTER EXERCISE: LETTER OF APPLICATION

Create a rough draft of your letter of application for work experience. Make sure it is no longer than one page and is laid out appropriately.

Your name and address

Date

Recipient's name and address

Salutation (i.e. Dear Sir/Madam)

SUBJECT HEADING (all caps and bold)

Body of letter – no more than three paragraphs

Complementary close

Signature

_____

Line under handwritten name
Name typed under the line with first letter capitals only
Enc. (if CV is attached)

Job Search Definitions

A *job description* consists of the job title, location, duties attached and any other special features of the post being advertised.

A *job specification* refers to the special qualities, qualifications and skills that are sought by an organisation. These usually do not appear in a newspaper advertisement. Candidates are encouraged to phone, check a company website or write to the organisation concerned for these details.

Job Search Strategies

There are a number of job-finding strategies open to someone actively seeking work. We will examine the following:
* Online job searches
* Networking
* Media advertisements
* Employment services
* Recruitment fairs
* Employment agencies
* Notice boards

Online Job Searches
The internet is an excellent source of job opportunities for jobseekers, as many employers advertise job vacancies through the web. Some relevant websites are:
* www.jobs.ie
* www.irishjobs.ie
* www.findajob.ie
* www.corporateskills.com
* www.hrmrecruit.com
* http://jobs.donedeal.ie
* www.monster.ie
* www.recruitireland.com
* www.overseasjobs.com

Networking

In the context of job-hunting, networking means using friends or family connections in the effort to secure a job. For example, assume that you are looking for work as a baker. Your aunt works for Mick the Baker at his Longford bakery and finds out that one of her workmates is about to retire. She could bring the prospect of a job vacancy arising soon in this bakery to your attention.

Media Advertisements

Employers frequently place job advertisements in the media to bring job vacancies to the attention of prospective employees. Depending on the nature of the job vacancy, these advertisements can be placed in:

* Local and/or national newspapers
* Local and/or national radio
* Relevant magazines

Receptionist Required

Receptionist required – Dun Laoghaire Hotel. Experience an advantage, fluent English essential. CV to info@anonymoushotel.ie.

Great Sous Chef Opportunity

Location: Cork
Job type: Full time
             Permanent
Contact: Seamus O'Neill

Are you a savvy sous chef seeking a great job opportunity?
With award-winning service and food, we offer customers an affordable yet high-quality dining experience. In order to maintain these high standards, we are looking to take on a bright and savvy sous chef responsible for managing and overseeing the preparation, cooking and presentation of food in our kitchen. We are offering the right person a fantastic opportunity to be part of a well-established business.

We are looking for a talented individual who wants to work in a fast-paced environment with a team who pride themselves on the quality of our service.

To successfully fill this role, you should have the following attitude, behaviours, skills and values:
* Strong knowledge of food and kitchen operations
* Approach food in a creative and passionate way
* Strong team-leading and motivational skills
* Good communication skills
* Excellent planning and organisational skills
* Willingness to learn, contribute and adapt to our in-house business model

The successful candidate will have at least five years' experience in a similar role. You will be a self-starter with the ability to lead, motivate and encourage a team of chefs.

Employment Services
The following are a few important employment service organisations that help to prepare and mentor prospective employees towards employment opportunities:
* Obair – The Local Employment Service Network (www.localemploymentservices.ie)
* Solas – The Further Education and Training Authority (www.solas.ie)
* Work Placement Programme (www.welfare.ie)
* Tús – a community work placement scheme providing short-term working opportunities (www.citizensinformation.ie)

Recruitment Fairs
A recruitment fair, also known as a job or career fair, is an event for employers and recruiters to meet with prospective jobseekers. Fairs usually include company or organisation tables or boxes where CVs can be collected and business cards can be exchanged. Examples of recruitment fairs are detailed on these websites:
* Jobs Expo (www.jobsexpo.ie)
* GradIreland (http://gradireland.com)
* Career Zoo (www.careerzoo.ie)

Employment Agencies

Employment agencies normally have an office in a town or city. These agencies have:

- A pool of jobseekers
- A range of companies that are seeking employee(s) on their books

A jobseeker visits the employment agency for a short interview and an assessment before being taken onto its books. Recruitment consultants then work to match their pool of jobseekers to their companies' open positions. Suitable candidates are shortlisted and put forward for an interview with potential employers.

Examples of employment agencies are:

- Careerwise Recruitment (www.careerwise.ie)
- CPL Recruitment (www.cpl.ie)
- Sigmar Recruitment (www.sigmarrecruitment.com)

Notice Boards

Notice boards are a cost-effective way for a company or organisation to advertise a vacancy. We are all familiar with open positions being advertised on shopping centre notice boards. Many colleges also have a job notice board on their campuses.

A word of advice: Don't wait until you have finished your course to apply for jobs. While you are on work experience, you should be actively engaged in searching for jobs and keeping an eye out for suitable positions that match your prospective qualifications.

Insurance Requirements for Work Experience

Most employers will look for proof of student insurance before you are accepted for work experience. Most course providers will provide this insurance cover for students with an accompanying letter stating the extent of coverage for any liability incurred. This varies depending on the course provider. You need to make sure that you are covered by insurance, either by the employer, the course provider or both.

How to Prepare for an Interview

You must prepare well for an interview with a prospective employer.

Workplace Background Analysis

Find out some information about the company or organisation that you are going to be interviewed by.
* What is the manager's or owner's name?
* What products or services are offered?
* How many people are employed at the organisation?
* How many branches are there, nationally or internationally?

Job Background Analysis

Find out what the job requirements are and what will be expected of you. It is favourably looked on if you telephone the manager who will be interviewing you in advance in order to find out this information if it is not otherwise readily available to you.

CV Audit

After the initial greeting, the starting point of every interview is an employer scan of the candidate's CV. Precisely identify your practical skills and where you learned them, your personal qualities and skills, your interpersonal skills and where you learned them and your unique selling point (USP), i.e. why you are the most suitable person for the job. Then link your skills (practical, personal and interpersonal) with the job you are being interviewed for.

In summary, you must:
* Research the nature of the job you are being interviewed for.
* Examine your skills, abilities and past work experience.
* Try to relate your skills, abilities and work experience to the needs of the job.

Speech

Anticipate likely questions by consulting with your family and friends. Summarise your answers to these anticipated questions. A confident delivery that shows evidence of planning is essential. Planning your speech is the key to good organisation. This will minimise any nervousness you may experience before the interview.

Body Language and Attire for Work/Appearance/Dress

Always remember that first impressions at interviews are lasting. It is important to:

- Dress appropriately (formal dress) for the interview.
- Pay attention to tidiness and good personal hygiene.
- Be aware of your body language, e.g. fidgeting, crossing your legs, slouching.
- Be aware of the importance of eye contact with the interviewer.

Interview Tips for Job Hunters

… employers have increasingly high standards and want to select the best. To prove that you are the best candidate, keep the following in mind.

CVs should be well presented, two pages long, with no spelling mistakes and highlight your skills and experience. Don't worry about getting your CV bound; it makes no difference to what is inside.

Check every avenue for details of job opportunities. Ask friends, relatives, former employers, look in the newspapers and on the internet.

If you don't hear back from companies, phone them and ask if you can come for an interview.

The standard of job interviews is high. Be honest in what you say and think of factual answers to questions like 'Tell us about yourself' (start with something recent, not your childhood); 'Describe a situation where you have had to deal with stress' (e.g. dealing with an angry person); 'Have you ever had to follow a set of written instructions?' (remember, if you have completed an aptitude test as part of the interview process, this is an example); 'Have you ever had to work with someone who let down the team?' (it takes all sorts – give an accurate example if you have had this experience but remember to mention that person's good points too).

If you are asked about dealing with changing circumstances, remember that flexibility at work is considered very important by employers in Ireland, so avoid describing something that 'wasn't in my job description'.

Never criticise a former employer at interview.

You may find yourself being asked the same questions by different interviewers in the same company. You still need to answer fully each time and be consistent. The interviewers will be comparing notes afterwards and consider consistency as a positive.

You need to show the employer that you are interested in them. Find out what you can about the company in advance – most companies will send you information if you contact them.

Prepare a list of questions to ask at interview, for example:
* Why has the vacancy arisen?
* What are your company's/department's goals for the next quarter/year?
* Do you have any plans to expand into new markets?
* What is your most successful product and why?
* What is your company culture – for example, do you work in teams?
* Is training provided? If you have certain skills that you could pass on to others in the company, will you be given that opportunity?
* Do employees meet socially?
* Does the company have links with the community, e.g. sponsoring charities, providing work placements for the unemployed?

And, finally … keep in touch with companies that you do meet, write a thank you letter after interviews even if you are rejected first time, ask for feedback and let them know you're interested in future opportunities. Ireland is very small and you are guaranteed to come across the same people again.

© Independent Newspapers

Selling Yourself: Getting through the Job Interview

The three key attributes towards landing that job are appearance, application and attention...

Academic qualifications are not enough in the days when the ability to sell oneself to a prospective employer is king. Many human resources managers look for other qualities in a person besides their basic qualifications when interviewing for a position.

Good appearance and communications skills are imperative. Some interviewers may also ask the applicant to undergo a psychometric test. This consists of a series of questions that can be used to analyse a candidate's ability and personality.

It involves a rapid personality questionnaire where the candidate is asked to answer eighty questions by determining how well particular adjectives apply to them.

A personality profile of the applicant is then compiled under the following five headings: extroversion, confidence, structural, tough-mindedness and conformity.

A concise curriculum vitae is essential. It shouldn't be more than two A4 pages and it should list your work history, education record and achievements as well as personal details such as leisure and sports interests. But remember, the employer doesn't have the time or inclination to wade through pages and pages of your background.

Research the company you are hoping to work for. Familiarise yourself with as much background as you can and have a few questions ready to ask about the company during your interview.

During the interview, be positive, show you are flexible and try to be as relaxed as possible. Rehearse the obvious questions, such as 'Why do you want to join us?' and 'Why did you leave your last job?'

Don't be afraid to sell yourself. Companies want people who are not afraid to show that they are dynamic and energetic, says Brendan Devine, recruitment specialist with ETC Consultants. Be confident without being cocky. There used to be a tendency to underestimate personal qualities but that has now changed and companies want people who are enthusiastic and energetic, he says.

Avoid extremes of dress or strong perfume, as they could result in an instant poor impression. Don't be taken in by a relaxed, easy-going manner.

Don't slouch in the chair or fidget. Be positive even if tricky or aggressive questions are thrown at you.

If asked about your previous job, do not criticise your former or current employers, as this can indicate a lack of loyalty which will count against you.

Finally, don't wait for the employer to get back to you with an answer. Apply for other jobs in the meantime.

© Independent Newspapers

Dress to Impress: First Impressions at Interviews Are Most Important

... The days of turning up for a one-on-one interview are over. The candidate is likely to undergo a psychometric test, role play and functional examinations in addition to a forty-five-minute interview.

'We would advise candidates to prepare well for their interview, find out as much as possible about the company and have a number of questions prepared,' said Mr McGennis.

Lack of preparation is one of the biggest criticisms of people going for interviews. 'Some people can appear too arrogant and others reply to questions with a "yes" or "no" instead of expanding on their answer.'

If a candidate is unsure about a dress code for an interview, be conservative and wear a suit and tie. It is better to be over-dressed. Be yourself, make eye contact and have positive thoughts.

© Independent Newspapers

Contract of Employment

All employers must provide new employees with a written statement (contract) of their terms and conditions of employment within two months of starting the job.

By law, the contract of employment must include the following details:
* Full name of the employer and the employee
* Full address of the employer
* Place of work
* Nature of work
* Commencement date of the employment
* Duration of the contract (either fixed or permanent)
* Rate or method of calculation of payment and pay reference period
* Payment intervals, e.g. weekly, monthly
* Annual leave and other paid leave entitlements
* Hours of work (including overtime)
* Details of rest periods and breaks
* Sick leave and pension arrangements, where applicable
* Notice requirements
* Reference to any collective agreement – this is an agreement between employers and employees which regulates the terms and conditions of employees, their duties and the duties of the employer
* Some employments require garda vetting before they start, e.g. crèche employees

The contract of employment should be signed and dated by both parties. The employer is also obliged to keep a copy of this for at least one year after the employee leaves the organisation.

It is recommended that the following terms are also incorporated into a contract of employment:
* A probationary period – the initial period of employment, during which the supervisor considers whether or not the employee is able to do the job effectively and if he or she should be retained

- Retirement details
- Provisions for lay-off and short time
- A flexibility clause
- Confidentiality clause – employees may be dealing with sensitive information
- Health and safety – this refers to the safety policy, which should be set out in the Safety Statement
- Disciplinary and grievance clauses
- Changes to conditions of employment
- Dress code – for example, a firm of solicitors may require both male and female employees to wear a white shirt/tie and black suits.

Source: IBEC

There is a sample contract of employment in Chapter 4 (pages 83–87).

Workplace Skills

There is a range of effective employability skills for the workplace, which must be acquired and mastered over a period of time. These can be broken into three separate categories: personal communication, interpersonal communication and technological communication skills.

Personal Communication Skills

- Written communications skills, e.g. report writing and form filling
- Oral communications skills – the ability to speak clearly in a formal manner
- Visual communication skills – making eye contact with colleagues, managers and clients or customers

Interpersonal Communication Skills

- Working in teams – the ability to function as team player
- Effective listening – the ability to listen well in all situations
- Formal/informal conversation skills – you can express yourself well in all situations
- Understanding non-verbal communication, e.g. body language

Technological Communication Skills

The ability to be comfortable working with:
- E-mail
- Social networking, e.g. Twitter or Facebook
- SMS – text messaging
- Skype, e.g. video phone calls over the internet

CHAPTER EXERCISE CHECKLIST

Make sure you have included all the exercises in this chapter in your learner's portfolio.

Chapter Exercise	Completed
List your personal, interpersonal and vocational skills and rate them	
Choose your three top talents or strengths	
List your top five interests and/or hobbies	
List five practical skills that you possess that you believe are relevant to your chosen career	
Explain how the personal, interpersonal and vocational skills that you have identified would be an asset to the organisation that you are applying to for work experience	
List your short-, medium- and long-term goals and respective action points for your work experience	
Create a rough draft of your CV	
Create a rough draft of your letter of application for work experience.	

What Needs to Be in the Learner's Portfolio?

Planning and Preparation Section
- A comprehensive personal and vocational skills audit and checklist
- A comprehensive career plan for a specific vocational area with a clear statement of learning goals and action points for the work experience
- Evidence of using a variety of job search strategies (preparations for interview, etc.)
- Curriculum vitae or personal statement
- Letter of application and statement of contractual obligations

Vocational Study

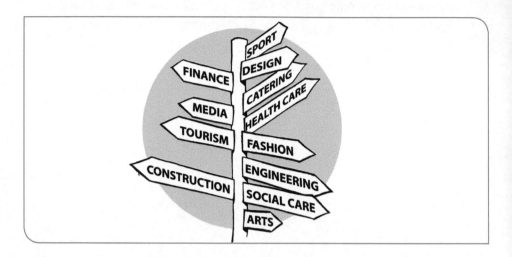

Key Issues Influencing Trends in the Vocational Area

In preparation for work experience, you need to recognise how changes in world events, globalisation, technology and population have affected or will have future effects on your chosen area of study and the industry you hope to gain work experience in.

Demographic changes, globalisation and rapid technological change are three major challenges facing Europe today. You should try to find out if your workplace and the industry that it is part of have been affected by these key issues.

Demographic Changes

'Demographics' is a shorthand term for population characteristics. It is the study of human population – how it is structured and how it changes. It examines how populations are dispersed and how the birth and death rates fluctuate over time, causing changing demographic structures in different countries.

The most frequently used demographic variables are age, gender, sexual orientation, family size, household size, family cycle, income, occupation, education, home ownership, socio-economic status, religion and nationality. In addition to demographic variables, a population can be segmented based on psychographic, geographic and behavioural variables.

The most noticeable changes in population (demographic shifts) in Ireland have been due to the following.

- **Economic shifts:** The Celtic Tiger years were marked by low unemployment rates and skills shortages. In response, employers tried to attract more women into the labour force and recruited workers from abroad. Increasingly flexible working arrangements, including job sharing, encouraged many people to take up or remain in employment.
- **An ageing population:** There will be a continuing need for additional care for the increasing number of elderly people. The Carer's Allowance has marked the beginning of this demographic shift in Ireland. The promotion of a flexible retirement age is also now evident.
- **Immigration:** Incoming migrants and refugees have come to Ireland because of war and/or economic instability in their countries of origin, e.g. Nigeria, the Congo and Eastern European countries such as Lithuania and Romania. However, since the recession in Ireland, many of these people have returned to their own countries or have gone to other countries in search of work.

- **Emigration:** Emigration out of Ireland is marked by a change to new and more varied destinations. At the beginning of the 20th century, Irish migrants were less likely to return home than any other Europeans. During the boom years returning migrants were a force to be reckoned with, but recession meant a growing number of people left the country in search of work. These changes in demographics obviously have an effect on employment as well as your expectations regarding who you may be working with or for while you are on work experience. The workplace has become increasingly multicultural, where you can appreciate and identify with other work colleagues' nationalities and cultures.

Globalisation

Globalisation means the impact that world events, world communications and world issues have on workplaces. In the 21st century, our reliance on international trade has both positive and negative effects.

- **Global communications:** The world wide web, e-mail, the internet, mobile phone technology and satellite communication have revolutionised world communication, allowing simple, quick access and exchange of global information, which can have both positive and negative effects on the workplace.
- **War and natural disasters:** Many products sold to the customer are imported, in particular oil, thus a change in world events, like the war in Iraq, can push up the price of oil and home heating oil in Ireland, causing the cost of living to rise. Natural disasters like tsunamis, hurricanes, landslides and earthquakes also affect people worldwide. For example, world oil prices increased substantially following Hurricane Katrina in 2005. Business transport costs were also severely affected by price increases in petrol and diesel.
- **Global economic changes:** In a global recession or economic downturn, Irish workers are affected by a fall in demand for certain products and by the decision of some companies to close down or to relocate to low-cost countries, resulting in job losses.
- **Global changes in technology:** New technological goods available abroad and imported into Ireland can make some companies' goods obsolete. These companies then have to diversify in order to stay competitive and to survive. For example, videos were replaced by DVDs and DVD sales are now falling because of downloads.

Rapid Technological Change

The development of smart mobility means that organisations want to employ staff with IT skills, which includes the need for a high level of knowledge and competence in the use of mobile devices. The ability to collect and manage large volumes of data (telematics applications) is also important now. This includes the ability to gather and analyse information (business intelligence) to be able to help organisations make better strategic decisions. In short, the employee should have good IT skills, including smart mobile device skills.

Other Factors Affecting Organisations and Industries – PEST Plus C

What is PEST plus C?

- **P means political factors** like government decisions or local authority decisions, e.g. taxation decisions or government spending decisions.
- **E means economic factors** like a global economic downturn triggered by terrorism and a fall in the value of stocks and shares because investors withdraw their funds. This usually causes a fall in the value of a country's currency and can cause unemployment.
- **S means social factors**, which describes social benefits or costs to a workplace. Examples of social benefits are car parking, bag packing and good customer service in retail outlets. Examples of social costs are pollution caused by a firm or an undesirable odour from a factory, for example a meat factory, all of which affect businesses and communities.
- **T means technological factors** (rapid technological change), where new technology speeds up the completion of tasks and may pose a risk to labour. Lack of up-to-date technology can be bad for productivity, resulting in higher labour costs.
- **C means competition factors**, describing the negative or positive effects the location or existence of the nearest competitor can have on a business. For example, large chain stores locating near small, specialised shops can cause the small shop to lose business. The larger outlet can avail of discounts and excellent credit terms (sometimes 90 days' credit) and pass these benefits on to the consumer in the form of lower prices. Examples of positive effects include hairdressers locating beside beauty salons – both may offer some similar services or products, but they also complement each other in many ways, thus helping both businesses.

Questions You Can Use

The following questions can be used to identify and explain key issues influencing your chosen industry or area of work experience (or vocational area). Both positive and negative effects should be noted.

1. Which industry is your chosen workplace part of?

For example, a small shop in the local shopping centre is part of the retail industry, whereas an insurance company or a bank are part of the financial services industry.

2. Demographic changes

Has this industry or organisation ever been affected by changes in population size or profile? For example, many non-nationals now work in the hotel and catering industry due to the multicultural nature of the workforce in Ireland in recent years.

3. Economic shifts and globalisation

Has this industry or organisation ever been affected by:
* World economic changes, e.g. the global downturn/recession, the change to the euro, the boom in the Irish economy, the credit crunch, changes in the housing market, the rising price of oil?
* World and national events, e.g. foot and mouth disease, swine flu, the war in Iraq, problems with terrorism, climate change?
* Natural disasters, e.g. drought, earthquakes, hurricanes, landslides, flooding?
* Global changes in technology?

4. Political issues

Has this industry or organisation ever been affected by:
* Changes in taxes?
* Ireland's membership of the European Union?
* Any other political decisions or lobby groups?

For example, vending machine suppliers had to alter their machines to suit the new euro currency, which would have been very costly. The smoking ban has affected pubs and restaurants and has created a need for outdoor rainproof spaces for smokers. Publicans have also had to buy patio heaters.

5. Social issues

Has this industry or organisation ever been affected by:

- Problems with pollution?
- Availability of car parking beside the workplace?
- Customer service and facilities?
- Kerb appeal?

6. Education level of potential employees

Does this industry or organisation have a minimum level of education that employees are expected to have in order to be employed?

7. Technological issues

Has this industry or organisation ever been affected by:

- New technology brought into the workplace, thereby creating a need for retraining?
- Lack of up-to-date technology?

8. Competition issues

Has this industry or organisation ever been affected by its nearest competitor or is there a niche market?

9. Future plans for the industry or organisation

Do you know if there are any changes planned for the future that will directly or indirectly affect the industry or organisation?

CHAPTER EXERCISE: KEY ISSUES INFLUENCING TRENDS

Answer the following questions to help put together your learner's portfolio.

1. Which industry is your chosen workplace part of?
2. How is the industry or organisation connected with your vocational area affected by the following key issues?
   - Demographic changes
   - Immigration/emigration
   - Economic shifts and globalisation
   - World and national events
   - Natural disasters (hurricanes, flooding, etc.)
   - Political issues

- Social issues
- Education level of potential employees
- Technological issues
- Competition issues
- Changes planned for the future

Summary

KEY CHALLENGES AND OPPORTUNITIES FACING PARTICULAR VOCATIONAL AREAS		
Sectors	Key Challenges	Opportunities
Overall economy	• There has been a complete collapse in construction employment. • There have been heavy job losses in retail too. • There has been a rise in long-term unemployment. *Source: Forfás Annual Report*	• Employment is growing in the ICT, business services, pharma, medical technologies, finance and agrifood sectors. • Agencies such as IDA Ireland, Enterprise Ireland, Udarás na Gaeltachta and Shannon Development continue to secure new investments, export growth and employment in client companies. • Ireland must remain competitive in order to continue to grow exports and create jobs. *Source: Forfás Annual Report*
Tourism	• The tourism industry was greatly affected by the economic downturn. • In less than three years, annual overseas visitors to Ireland dropped by 2 million and associated revenue fell by over €1.2 billion. • There was a modest recovery in 2011, which saw growth for the first time since 2007. *Source: Irish Tourist Industry Confederation (ITIC)*	• The Gathering Ireland 2013, a year-long tourism initiative, reported that 250,000 to 275,000 overseas visitors to Ireland travelled here specifically because of a Gathering, or because of the Gathering, in 2013. • The growth in visitor numbers directly attributable to the Gathering is estimated to be worth approximately €170 million in revenue. This was delivered within the Gathering's approved budget of €13 million from the Department for Transport, Tourism and Sport. *Source: www.thegatheringireland.com*

Healthcare, nursing	• There are long waiting lists for acute hospital care. • There are also long waiting times and poor conditions in A&E departments, including a high number of patients on trolleys. • By 2041, the population of over-65s in Ireland will have increased by 167%. The increase for those aged over 85 will be 350%. Care and sheltered accommodation for these people needs to be planned and put in place. This will create challenges for the nursing home sector. • Laws concerning home births and insufficient insurance cover prevent registered midwives from assisting legally at home births. *Source: www.bdo.ie*	• Opportunities for jobs in healthcare and nursing are increasing. The requirement for appropriately qualified staff for different areas of healthcare includes FETAC/QQI qualifications at Levels 5 and 6. • The economic crisis has led to a higher incidence of ill health and a growing dependence on the public healthcare system by people experiencing unemployment and reduced incomes. • There is a need now to meet the higher dependency and increased acuity needs of older people. • Jobs will likely be available in the nursing home sector as well as in areas like caring for older people and childcare (see www.inmo.ie).
Pharmacy/ medical	• According to PharmaChemical Ireland, 'patents for major "blockbuster" drugs are expiring, emerging replacement products coming through the research pipeline are lacking, and the industry is opening up to generic competition'. • Ireland is vulnerable to these changes because so many of the world's largest medicines are produced here. • Cost competitivness is a major issue. *Source: www.irishexporters.ie*	• FETAC/QQI graduates can progress to studying pharmacy at the higher education level. • Opportunities for more jobs are likely for the future, as the age profile of the population has changed. People are living longer and will need pharmacy services into the future.

Childcare	• According to Early Childhood Ireland, 'facilities are being forced to cut back on their services or their range of services in order to survive'. • Budget changes to the ECCE, CETS and CCS schemes will impact negatively on childcare facilities as well as on the families that depend on such facilities. *Source: www.earlychildhoodireland.ie*	• Many childcare businesses are innovating by restructuring their services and providing additional services, such as out-of-school services for the summer holidays and midterm breaks. • The government has established a quality assurance policy. From September 2015, all staff in existing services must have a Level 5 qualification in early childhood care and education and team leaders will have to have a Level 6 qualification (or equivalent). • Opportunities also exist for childcare workers to up-skill and thus strengthen public confidence in childcare services. *Source: www.earlychildhoodireland.ie*
Media, TV/radio, multimedia	• 'Media agencies have had to move very fast to absorb the way that digital and, most importantly, social media have become part of our lives.' • 'The staff of a media agency today will include roles that simply didn't exist a decade ago: search specialists, social media technology experts and content creators to name but three.' *Source: www.mediacom.com*	• 'The consumer appetite for digital content continues to grow – and change – at a staggering pace. Media consumption has not just gone digital; it's connected.' • 'As consumers continue to enhance and replace traditional media consumption with digital experiences, incumbent media companies face a potential revenue challenge. Equally, there are new revenue opportunities available to companies in this regard.' *Source: www.ibm.com*

Print journalism	<ul><li>Challenges include the closure of print organisations and the move to online journalism, the rush and strain of newsroom practices, the need for self-belief and a questioning mind and not to be afraid to express one's individuality (subject to editorial and corporate guidelines).</li><li>Concerns exist about the future of the media and journalism industry and the impact of developments in technologies and social media like Facebook and Twitter.</li><li>The shifting of organisational structures is also of concern, as downturns and upswings in economies happen and you need to plan to address these changes by retraining.</li><li>There is an increasing need for multitasking (e.g if you are trained as a print journalist you have a better chance of getting a job if you are also trained as a radio presenter).</li><li>You will need to be able to distinguish between genuine journalistic content and PR-driven information that might be skewed to suit the advertisers.</li><li>Be aware of the need for accountability to the public and the risk of being sued if you intentionally or unintentionally defame a person's character by printing or broadcasting incorrect information about a person or company.</li></ul>	<ul><li>More than 80% of Irish adults still read a newspaper, which is one of the highest percentages in Europe.</li><li>Publishers and editors have a rich store of local content and community knowledge, loyalty and contacts that, if appropriately mined, can secure a profitable future.</li></ul> *Source: www.irishexaminer.com*

Advertising	• 'According to advertisers, too much time is spent focusing on all the different technology and distribution channels than on content. How you connect seems more important than what you say, and this is a challenge. It is easy to forget that the message and feel are more important than the distribution vehicle. It's creativitiy that differentiates and builds relationships, not technology alone. Marketeers that can harness and straddle that bridge are the ones who will succeed.' • 'Data overload is also a challenge. Based on clients wanting clear, cost-effective, measurable and accountable routes to their customers, it is challenging to achieve this based on media budget restrictions.' *Source: www.kdnine.com*	• 'There are new revenue opportunities for media companies and advertisers as similarities between broadcast and digital video advertising grow.' • 'Now all broadcast information can be received on mobile devices.' • 'Economic recovery is evident, particularly in the area of outdoor advertising, with more realistic expectations regarding value for money.' • 'New, improved creative approaches to advertising exist, allowing advertisers to adopt new, improved modern strategies like smart marketing using social networking, etc. and to devise campaigns that are innovative, easily accessible and stimulating for the customer.' *Source: http://blogs.adobe.com*

New media	• Advances in digital interactivity mean that those interested in media must gain advanced skills in areas such as computer multimedia, software/video gaming and mobile phone technology.	• Job opportunities in new media are widely available due to the rapid nature of changing technology. These jobs include digital media co-ordinators as managers of company pages on social media sites like Facebook and Twitter, where customer relations, branding and knowledge of how to manage company web activity would be needed; administrators of online forums (company chat rooms); online business development managers; smart online marketing managers; digital project managers; and e-recruitment managers or administrators. • You need to have a good working knowledge of the effective use and benefit of digital media in business along with practical experience in sales and marketing.
Agriculture, horticulture	• The horsemeat controversy of 2013 was a major scandal. • Food security will continue to be a challenge. *Source: www.agriculture.gov.ie*	• The global economic crisis combined with the severe difficulties in Ireland's own economy have highlighted the importance of the agrifood sector. • 'Opportunities can be built on, as Ireland has a tradition of exporting food and animal products as well as live animals to many international markets, with a mix of global food ingredient companies co-existing alongside smaller artisan companies and live exporting businesses, resulting in an €8 billion agrifood export sector, based on doing business with many of the leading retailers across Europe.' *Source: www.agriculture.gov.ie*

Hair and beauty	The top five challenges of owning a salon include: <ul><li>**Rent:** Rents are high for small businesses.</li><li>**Fees:** Many salons buy state-of-the-art equipment to attract the appropriate clients.</li><li>**Cash flow for small businesses:** Banks are not lending as much in recent times following the recession.</li><li>**Reliant on return business and staying competitive:** Keeping customers happy.</li><li>**Keeping up with trends in hair and in beauty:** Products might be expensive, which attracts clients too.</li></ul> *Source: www.cashierlive.com*	<ul><li>Barbering, upstyles and other specialised areas in hairdressing are proving more and more popular. Job opportunities in these areas are developing.</li><li>Beauty salons are constantly learning new ways to assist with relaxation and to help clients with problem skin (anti-ageing skincare, eye enhancers, etc.).</li><li>'More and more beauty industry growth is being powered by the fields of science and technology, using broader innovations to create and promote new beauty products' (source: www.gcimagazine.com).</li><li>'A wide range of digital tools . . . is available to brands that want to capture the attention of consumers, turn their visits into purchases, or increase their loyalty' (source: premiernews.com).</li><li>Opportunities exist to learn more by keeping up with trends in the industry and in so doing to make more money. See what others in the industry are doing by attending hair and beauty shows and entering competitions to gain a better reputation and to attract customers. See www.irishbeauty.ie and www.irishhairdfed.com.</li></ul>

Art	• According to Visual Artists Ireland, 'Many challenges exist for artists in Ireland. Many artists earn a living or supplement their income through working in arts administration or third-level education.'	• Further education art courses can allow you to progress to degree level. Engaging in further study – whether specialist training, postgraduate education or professional development programmes – gives you the chance to develop your practice through enhancing your skills and/or through critical engagement with others. • A postgraduate diploma or masters degree is becoming a minimum requirement. • The rapid pace of technological change in areas such as new media means that updating your skills can be advantageous.
Accounting	• According to Accountancy Ireland, 'the challenges and opportunities facing accountants, especially those working in the banking sector, are extensive, with smaller accountancy firms feeling the impact of economic instability'. • Due to what accountants call misdirected criticism of financial reporting and audit, new challenges exist to create ways in which auditor communication can be improved to allow for greater transparency in the public eye. Accountants need to have a working knowledge of areas that have become noteworthy, including debt forgiveness and insolvency. They also need to be prepared for the radical changes taking place in the areas of banking and finance.	• There are opportunities to secure work in accountancy in other countries, including Australia. • Diversify by specialising in areas of insolvency or dealing with redundancies. • Some accountants have evolved into partnerships, thereby increasing personal brand awareness and allowing for the sharing of expertise.

| Small business set-up | • Challenges facing SMEs include finance, promotion, sales and marketing, HR, IT and production. Larger businesses have internal supports like departments and specialised personnel (group thinking) to assist them, but SMEs usually don't.
• Problems with credit, such as getting loans or cash flow restrictions due to the credit squeeze.
• Competition from larger competitors that can avail of bulk buying and large discounts and thus charge lower prices to customers. | • Enterprise Ireland can provide financial support towards the cost of establishing, growing and expanding your business. The funding is typically a mix of equity and grants and is specifically intended to meet expenses in the areas of research and design, training, job creation and acquisition of capital assets (source: www.enterprise-ireland.com).
• Business start-up grants are available. There are a number of schemes available to assist new and developing enterprises in Ireland, such as City and County Enterprise Boards and capital grants, employment grants and feasbility grants (source: www. enterpriseboards.ie).
• SMEs need to establish a niche offering (products or services) that is independent and well marketed or one that complements other businesses.
• 'Shop local' initiatives have helped local businesses to attract customers from the local area (see www. smeblog.ie). |

| Retailing | • SMEs have been severely hit by the recession.
• Many have had to close, while others have had to shed staff to survive and many will have to diversify to survive. This includes retail outlets.
• The lack of availability of cash (bank lending has been cut) has caused cash flow problems for organisations.
• Rents and rates have also been a major challenge for retail and small businesses in Ireland. | • Retailing is interlinked with small business. However, the local corner shop is no longer a common entity. Increasingly, retail parks that have an effective marketing strategy tend to attract shoppers, such as the Cresent Shopping Centre in Limerick.
• Consumer spending is expected to rise from 2014 onwards, which will help create more jobs in retailing.
• The national representative body for the retail sector, Retail Ireland, has a new strategy for retail with a potential for 40,000 new jobs (see www.retailireland.ie). |

CHAPTER EXERCISE CHECKLIST

Make sure you have included all the exercises in this chapter in your learner's portfolio.

Chapter Exercise	Completed
Which industry is your chosen workplace part of?	
How is the industry or organisation connected with your vocational area affected by the listed key issues?	

What Needs to Be in the Learner's Portfolio?

Vocational Study Section
A profile of the vocational area, to include:
• Evidence of analysing the key challenges and opportunities facing the particular vocational area, such as demographic change, immigration/emigration, economic shifts, education level of potential employees and new technologies
• Career opportunities
• Future skills needs

CHAPTER 4

Work and the Law: Basic Rights and Responsibilities of Employees and Employers

"OK, OK, we'll give you better conditions!"

LEARNING OUTCOMES

- DETERMINE EMPLOYER AND EMPLOYEE RESPONSIBILITIES.
- EXAMINE WORK-RELATED HEALTH AND SAFETY ISSUES AND THE RELEVANT LEGISLATION.
- INVESTIGATE EQUALITY-RELATED ISSUES AND THE RELEVANT LEGISLATION.
- DETERMINE THE ROLE OF UNIONS IN THE WORKPLACE.
- EXAMINE OTHER KEY EMPLOYMENT REGULATION LEGISLATION.
- OUTLINE A RANGE OF ESSENTIAL EMPLOYMENT RIGHTS.
- IDENTIFY KEY INDUSTRIAL RELATIONS BODIES.

Employer and Employee Responsibilities

Employers and employees have responsibilities to one another.

The main responsibilities of an **employer** are to:
* Provide work.
* Pay employees at an appropriate wage level in line with minimum wage legislation.
* Recognise equality issues and equal opportunities related to the workplace based on:
    * Gender
    * Civil status (single, married, separated, divorced or widowed)
    * Family status (this refers to the parent of a person under 18 years or the resident primary carer or parent of a person with a disability)
    * Sexual orientation
    * Religion
    * Age (does not apply to a person under 16)
    * Disability
    * Race
    * Membership of the Traveller community
* Make sure employees are insured in the workplace (most businesses are covered by full public liability insurance).
* Adhere to the safety, health and welfare legislation.
* Respect employee representation by their trade unions.
* Inform workers of their rights regarding their terms of employment by providing employees with a written statement of these terms.
* Provide workers with appropriate minimum notice before the termination of a contract of employment.

The main responsibilities of an **employee** are to:
* Be available for work and provide a good service.
* Obey orders from superiors or employers.
* Exercise their work duties with diligence and an acceptable level of efficiency.
* Maintain confidentiality regarding company information.
* Be willing to compensate the employer for any damage caused or wrongful act committed.

What Is Employment Legislation?

Employment legislation is a law or body of laws enacted to protect the rights of the employer and/or the employee. In this book, we will focus on employment legislation that deals with:
- Health, safety and welfare at work
- Equality
- Union representation
- Other employment regulation issues (pay, annual leave, maternity leave and parental leave)

Health, Safety and Welfare at Work

The primary legislation providing for the health and safety of people at work is the **Safety, Health and Welfare at Work Act 2005–2007.**

The duties of employees under this Act include:
- Taking reasonable care to protect the health and safety of themselves and of other people in the workplace
- Not engaging in improper behaviour that will endanger themselves or others
- Not being under the influence of drink or drugs in the workplace
- Undergoing any reasonable medical or other assessment if requested to do so by the employer
- Reporting any defects in the workplace or equipment that might be a danger to health and safety

Employers have a duty to ensure their employees' health, safety and welfare at work as far as is reasonably practicable. In order to prevent workplace injuries and ill health, an employer is required, among other things, to:
- Provide and maintain a safe workplace that uses safe plant and equipment
- Prevent risks from the use of any article or substance and from exposure to physical agents, noise and vibration
- Prevent any improper conduct or behaviour likely to put the safety, health and welfare of employees at risk
- Provide instruction and training to employees on health and safety
- Provide protective clothing and equipment to employees
- Appoint a competent person as the organisation's Safety Officer

Every employer is required to carry out a risk assessment for the workplace to identify any hazards present, assess the risks arising from such hazards and identify the steps to be taken to deal with such risks.

A safety statement must be prepared by the employer, which is based on the risk assessment. The statement should also contain the details of people in the workforce who are responsible for safety issues. Employees should be given access to this statement and employers should review it on a regular basis.

Employers should carry out separate risk assessments for pregnant employees and employees who are under 18 years of age. The latter assessment should be carried out before the young person is employed.

Employees should be informed by their employer about any risks that require wearing protective equipment. The employer should provide protective equipment (such as protective clothing, headgear, footwear, eyewear and/or gloves) together with training on how to use it, where necessary. An employee has a duty to take reasonable care for his or her own safety and to use any protective equipment supplied. The protective equipment should be provided free of charge to employees if it is intended for use at the workplace only. Employees should usually be provided with their own personal equipment. The correct use of computers is an important health and safety consideration for employers and employees. The Health and Safety Authority sets out guidelines for correct computer use on their website (www.hsa.ie).

All accidents in the workplace should be reported to the employer, who should record the details of the incident. Proper safeguards should be put into place to eliminate the risk of violence as far as possible and the employee should be provided with appropriate means of minimising the remaining risk, e.g. security glass.

Equality at Work

Equality legislation exists to safeguard against discrimination. A person is said to be discriminated against if he or she is treated less favourably than another is, has been or would be treated in a comparable situation on any of the following nine grounds:

- Gender
- Civil status (single, married, separated, divorced or widowed)
- Family status (this refers to the parent of a person under 18 years or the resident primary carer or parent of a person with a disability)
- Sexual orientation
- Religion
- Age (does not apply to a person under 16)
- Disability
- Race
- Membership of the Traveller community

There are two distinct pieces of legislation that set out important rights for people and outlaw discrimination when it occurs. The **Employment Equality Acts 1998–2011** and the **Equal Status Acts 2000–2011** outlaw discrimination in employment, vocational training, advertising, collective agreements and the provision of goods and services. Specifically, goods and services include professional or trade services; health services; access to accommodation and education; and facilities for banking, transport and cultural activities.

Equality Issues and Definitions

- **Positive action:** In recent years, employers have been encouraged to establish policies and procedures to show that they are taking reasonable steps to demonstrate their commitment to equality and to avoid discrimination in the work environment. Usually these policies and procedures are documented in the form of an equal opportunities policy and grievance procedures (employee complaints procedures) in an employee handbook, which is usually available from an organisation's human resources department. Employers also promote positive action by organising anti-racism, anti-harassment and anti-bullying training for staff. The aim is to comply with equality legislation and to avoid discrimination.
- **Ethnic group:** An ethnic group is defined by a common identity, kinship, ancestry, culture, history or tradition. For example, the Travelling community is Ireland's largest ethnic minority, although during the Celtic Tiger years, immigration created a multiethnic Ireland. Ethnic groups can

sometimes be defined based on having a common religion or language, such as Protestants and Catholics in Northern Ireland.

- **Ethnicity:** The identity with or membership of a particular racial, national or cultural group and observance of that group's customs, beliefs and language. Ethnic groups can exist comfortably as part of a different race, for example the Chinese community in New York City.
- **Racial and religious equality:** Promoting equality among the races and respecting and understanding cultural diversity, religion and customs.
- **Gender equality:** Promoting equality between the sexes.
- **Age equality:** Promoting equality for people aged over 50.
- **Disability equality:** Promoting equality for the disabled.
- **Sexual orientation equality:** Promoting equality for non-heterosexual workers (gays and lesbians as well as transgender).
- **Sexual harassment:** Defined as 'unwanted conduct of a sexual nature or other conduct based on sex affecting the dignity of women and men at work'.
- **Bullying:** Verbal, physical or psychological aggression engaged in by an employer against employees or by an employee or a group of employees against another employee. It can take the form of intimidation, isolation, victimisation, exclusion, shouting, abusive behaviour, constant criticism or nagging, verbal threats, physical threats, humiliation, excessive controlling behaviour, unreasonable behaviour or task assignment, or posters, banners, e-mails and emblems that cause offence.
- **Equality regarding marital and family status:** Promoting equality for men, women and children in the home.

Equal Opportunities in Employment

Employers are legally obliged to adhere to the existing equality legislation when hiring and employing staff, whether they are full time or part time. When you are an employee or a prospective candidate, your employer cannot discriminate against you, as follows.

- **The recruitment procedure:** Having a discriminatory manner or asking discriminatory questions during the interview (you have a right to information through an equality officer if you suspect discrimination has or is taking place).
- **Access to employment:** Having different entry requirements for you compared to other applicants.

- **Conditions of employment:** Unequal terms of employment and work conditions, overtime, shift work, transfers or dismissals (except remuneration).
- **Training and experience:** Your employer must provide the same opportunities or facilities for employment counselling and training and work experience as those offered to other employees in similar circumstances.
- **Promotion or re-grading:** Access to promotional opportunities must be allowed by your employer as is allowed to similarly qualified or other candidates.

Union Representation in the Workplace

Employees have a constitutional right to join a union. A union can provide an important source of information and protection in relation to employment matters as well as negotiating with the employer for better pay and conditions. There are three main types of union:

- **Craft unions:** The skilled category, e.g. Irish Print Union.
- **White collar unions:** Professional, office and service occupations, e.g. Teachers Union of Ireland (TUI).
- **General unions:** Semi-skilled and unskilled workers, e.g. Services, Industrial, Professional and Technical Union (SIPTU).

The Irish Congress of Trade Unions (ICTU) is the umbrella organisation for most of the bigger unions of workers in Ireland and represents employees at social partnership talks, i.e. talks between government representatives, employer representatives (such as IBEC or SFA) and other interested groups (such as Age Action Ireland). Pay structures and work conditions are recommended and negotiated. A national wage agreement is usually secured for workers, such as the **Haddington Road Agreement.**

There is no legal obligation on an employer to negotiate with a union on behalf of an employee member unless previously agreed. This does not prevent a dispute about trade union recognition from being a lawful dispute.

Dismissal for trade union activity or membership is automatically unfair under the **Unfair Dismissals Acts 1977–2007.** An employee dismissed in such circumstances does not require any particular length of service in the job in order to bring a case in this instance under the law.

Other Employment Regulation Issues

Working Hours

Guidelines for the maximum working hours are set out in the **Organisation of Working Time Act 1997**. Most employees cannot work more than 48 hours in an average working week.

Pay

The amount of pay received for working is a matter of agreement between the employer and employee. Under the **National Minimum Wage Act 2000**, most employees are entitled to a minimum wage. Since 1 July 2011 the national minimum wage for an experienced adult employee is **€8.65 per hour**.

Annual Leave

Annual leave or holidays from work is set down in legislation and in the contract of employment. The **Organisation of Working Time Act 1997** provides for a basic annual paid leave entitlement of four weeks, although an employee's contract could give greater rights.

It must be noted that the periods of leave provided for by legislation are the minimum entitlements only; an employer and employee may agree to additional entitlements. Holiday pay or pay in respect of annual leave is paid in advance at the normal weekly rate.

Maternity Leave

Female employees who become pregnant while in employment are entitled to take maternity leave. The entitlement to a basic period of maternity leave from employment extends to all female employees (including casual workers), regardless of how long you have been working for the organisation or the number of hours worked per week. You can also avail of additional unpaid maternity leave. **The Maternity Protection Act 1994** and the **Maternity Protection (Amendment) Act 2004** provide the statutory minimum entitlements in relation to maternity at work, including maternity leave.

Since 1 March 2007, there are entitlements to 26 weeks' maternity leave together with an option of a further 16 weeks' additional unpaid maternity leave.

Under the **Maternity Protection (Amendment) Act 2004**, at least two weeks' leave have to be taken before the end of the week of the baby's expected birth and at least four weeks after. You can decide how you would like to take the remaining weeks.

A woman on maternity leave is entitled to pay and superannuation during the leave, depending on the terms of the contract of employment. Employers are not obliged to pay women on maternity leave. Mothers on maternity leave may qualify for Maternity Benefit, which is a Department of Social Protection payment, provided sufficient PRSI contributions have been made. An employee's contract, however, could provide for additional rights to payment during the leave period. For example, the employee could receive full pay less the amount of Maternity Benefit payable.

Parental Leave

The **Parental Leave Act 1998**, as amended by the **Parental Leave (Amendment) Act 2006**, allows parents in Ireland to take parental leave from employment in respect of certain children. The amount of parental leave available to each parent per child is 18 weeks.

Leave can be taken in respect of a child up to eight years of age and both parents have an equal separate entitlement to parental leave.

An employee is not entitled to pay from his or her employer while on parental leave, nor is the employee entitled to any social welfare payment equivalent to Maternity Benefit. Taking parental leave does not affect your other employment rights.

Contract of Employment

The **Terms of Employment (Information) Acts 1994 and 2001** require employers to provide a written statement setting out particulars of the terms of employment to employees within the first two months of the commencement of employment.

The following is a sample contract of employment.

This contract of employment is made the _____ day of _____ 20___ between (Employee name) _____ _____ of (Employee address) _____ _____, hereinafter known as 'the Employee', and (Employer name) _____ of (Employer address) _____ _____, hereinafter known as 'the Company'.

The regulations and conditions of employment as set out herein will be deemed to constitute a 'contract of employment', in fulfilment of current employment legislation. All Employees will be required to sign at the space provided at the end of these conditions, agreeing to adhere to the Company's conditions of employment.

(i)   **Date of Commencement:** _____ day of _____ 20__.

(ii) **Place of Work:** The Employee shall be based for the time being at _____.

(iii) **Job Function:** The Employee shall be employed as _____ and he/she shall also be required to carry out associated functions as the Company may from time to time require.

(iv) **Probationary Period:** A probationary period of _____ weeks/ months will apply. A letter notifying the Employee of his/her appointment to permanent staff will be issued at the end of a successfully completed probationary period.

(v) Hours of Work: The hours of work shall be _____ a.m. to _____ p.m., or a total number of ____ hours per week, as shall be set out by the Company from time to time but in any event shall at all times be in compliance with the provisions of the Organisation of Working Time Act 1997.

(vi) Salary: The Employee's annual salary shall be €_____. Salary will be reviewed _____. Payment shall be by direct debit into the Employee's bank account, the account details to be provided by the Employee to the Company on the execution of the within contract.

(vii) Annual Leave: In addition to the nine public holidays, twenty working days' holiday is allowed during a full calendar year, 1 January to 31 December, in accordance with the provisions of the Organisation of Working Time Act 1997.

Upon termination of employment, the entitlement will be a proportion of the appropriate annual holiday based on the number of calendar months completed during the calendar year of departure, subject to a minimum period of notice under the Minimum Notice and Terms of Employment Acts 1973–1991.

(viii) Absence through Illness: The manager must be notified as soon as possible after 9:00 a.m. in all cases where a member of the staff is unable to attend at the place of work. A medical certificate is required if absence extends beyond three consecutive days and should cover the period until the staff member is declared fit for work. Dental appointments, visits to the doctor, etc. should, where possible, be arranged outside working hours.

(ix) Compassionate Leave: Compassionate leave will be at the discretion of the management but, in the case of near relatives, will be such as to allow full attendance at funeral services.

(x) Leave of Absence: Approval and duration of unpaid personal leave shall be at the discretion of the Company.

(xi) Grievance Procedure: The Company is most anxious that legitimate grievances raised by an Employee are expeditiously and fairly resolved. Any member of staff who has a grievance relating to his/her employment should discuss it with the Company.

(xii) Dismissal: The Company hopes that it will not become necessary to dismiss an Employee. However, it must be understood that there are certain breaches of company rules for which, after the facts have been ascertained, an Employee may be summarily dismissed or suspended, without pay, pending further investigations. In such an event, an Employee will be afforded a full right of representation of his/her case to the Company before a final decision is made. Continued failure to adhere to normal Company requirements, including timekeeping, attendance, job performance, confidentiality in relation to all the Company's affairs and general conduct, will result in an Employee being subject to the following procedure:

- The Employee will receive a verbal warning.
- The Employee will receive a first formal written warning advising that continued failure to improve on the specific aspect of performance will lead to disciplinary action.
- The Employee will receive a final formal written warning.
- The Employee will be suspended for a fixed period, without pay.
- The Employee will be dismissed in the event of it becoming absolutely clear that no, or insufficient, improvement on the aspect of performance is forthcoming.

At all times the Employer will abide by procedural fairness under current employment legislation when dealing with dismissals from the Company.

(xiii) Notice Periods: Staff who wish to terminate their employment with the Company are expected to give the following notice:

All Employees on probation – 1 week
Employees appointed to permanent staff – 1 month
Senior/management staff – 2 months

or in times of conflict in accordance with Section 4 of the Minimum Notice and Terms of Employment Act 1973. Notwithstanding the foregoing, the Company may, at its discretion, waive its right to notice.

(xiv) **Standard of Dress:** All Employees are expected to conform to an acceptable standard of dress to ensure that the image as presented to customers, colleagues and associates is in keeping with the proper professional approach of the Company.

Where uniform is required dress, no personal additions will be made to the uniform, and it shall be cleaned by the Employee for the duration of their contract.

(xv) **Confidentiality:** The Employee will not, during or at any time after the termination of your employment, disclose to any person or persons (except to senior Employees of the Company) nor use for your own benefit any confidential information that you may receive or obtain in relation to the affairs of the Company or its clients.

(xvi) **Alteration to Terms of Employment:** Any alterations in the regulations of employment affecting staff individually will be notified by a letter or memorandum, but any general alteration will be communicated in a circular to be seen by all members of staff.

I agree to be bound by the regulations and conditions of employment as contained in the foregoing.

Signed:

_____

Date:

_____

Signed for and on behalf of The Company:

Signed:

_____

Date:

_____

Employment Rights and Industrial Relations Bodies

Over the past few years, the government has been working on the **Workplace Relations Reform Programme.** The aim of this programme is to deliver a world-class workplace relations service and employment rights framework that serves the needs of employers and employees and provides maximum value for money.

The specific objectives of the programme include:
* Promoting maximum compliance with employment law
* Providing a single authoritative source of information on employment law
* Ensuring employers and employees understand their respective rights and obligations
* Providing access to services within a reasonable timeframe
* Simplifying access to and navigation of the employment dispute resolution processes
* Resolving grievances and disputes as close to the workplace as possible
* Resolving workplace grievances and disputes as early as possible after they arise
* Providing credible enforcement and an effective, risk-based inspection regime
* Providing simple, accessible, independent, fair and timely adjudication
* Providing a simple, accessible, independent, fair and timely means of appeal

The project is looking to develop a two-tier workplace relations structure by merging the activities of the National Employment Rights Authority (NERA), the Labour Relations Commission (LRC), the Equality Tribunal and some functions of the Labour Court and the Employment Appeals Tribunal (EAT) into a new body called the **Workplace Relations Commission (WRC).** Some of the functions of the Employment Appeals Tribunal will be incorporated into an expanded Labour Court.

Details of this new workplace relations structure can be found on the Workplace Relations website (www.workplacerelations.ie).

Summary

The following legislation defines employee rights and employer obligations in the workplace:

* Adoptive Leave Act 2005
* Carer's Leave Act 2001
* Data Protection Acts 1988–2003
* Employees (Provision of Information and Consultation) Act 2006
* Employment Permits Act 2006
* Equality Act 2004 and Employment Equality Act 1998
* Freedom of Information Acts 1997–2003
* Maternity Protection (Amendment) Act 2004
* Minimum Notice and Terms of Employment Acts 1973–2001
* National Minimum Wage Act 2000
* Organisation of Working Time (Records) (Prescribed Form and Exemptions) Regulations 2001
* Organisation of Working Time Act 1997
* Parental Leave (Amendment) Act 2006
* Payment of Wages Act 1991
* Protection of Employees (Fixed-Term Work) Act 2003
* Protection of Employees (Part-Time Work) Act 2001
* Protection of Employees on Transfer of Undertakings Regulations Act 2003
* Protection of Employment (Exceptional Collective Redundancies and Related Matters) Act 2007
* Protection of Employment (Temporary Agency Work) Act 2012
* Protection of Young Persons (Employment) Act 1996
* Redundancy Payments Acts 1967–2007
* Safety, Health and Welfare at Work Act 2005
* Terms of Employment (Information) Acts 1994 and 2001
* Unfair Dismissals Acts 1977–2007

CHAPTER EXERCISE

1. List an employer's main obligations.
2. List an employee's main obligations.
3. Write down what you know about health and safety in the workplace and the main legal Act underpinning it.
4. Write down what you know about employment equality and the two main legal Acts underpinning it.
5. Outline four basic rights of an employee and the respective legislation that helps to safeguard these rights.
6. List the objectives of the reform programme put in place by the government to oversee workplace relations.

CHAPTER EXERCISE CHECKLIST

Make sure you have included all the exercises in this chapter in your learner's portfolio.

Chapter Exercise	Completed
List the responsibilities of an employer.	
List the responsibilities of an employee.	
Outline your knowledge of health and safety in the workplace and the relevant legislation.	
Outline your knowledge of equality issues in the workplace and the relevant legislation.	
Summarise four basic employee rights and the underpinning legislation.	
List the objectives of the workplace relations reform programme.	

What Needs to Be in the Learner's Portfolio?

Vocational Study Section
* A summary of the basic rights and responsibilities of employees and employers in a particular work, organisational or institutional context

We wish to acknowledge the help of the Citizens Information Board (www. citizensinformation.ie) in producing this chapter.

CHAPTER 5

The Work Placement

"I wondered if you could stay on after your week's work experience?"

LEARNING OUTCOMES

- INCLUDE AN ACCOUNT OF DAILY PERFORMANCE, WORK EXPERIENCE DIARY/ACCOUNT OF WORK DONE, LEARNING AND CHALLENGES ENCOUNTERED.
- INCLUDE EVIDENCE OF THE EFFECTIVE PARTICIPATION AND PRACTICE OF EMPLOYABILITY SKILLS WHILE ON WORK EXPERIENCE.
- INCLUDE EVIDENCE OF HAVING OBSERVED GOOD TIMEKEEPING.
- INCLUDE EVIDENCE OF HAVING WORKED INDEPENDENTLY WHILE UNDER GENERAL DIRECTION.
- INCLUDE EVIDENCE OF HAVING MET DEADLINES RELATIVE TO THE VOCATIONAL AREA.
- INCLUDE EVIDENCE OF HAVING TAKEN CARE WITH YOUR PERSONAL PRESENTATION.
- INCLUDE EVIDENCE OF IMPROVED OR NEWLY LEARNED COMMUNICATION SKILLS.
- INCLUDE EVIDENCE OF HAVING ADHERED TO HEALTH AND SAFETY AND OTHER BUSINESS AND LEGAL REGULATIONS.

You need to familiarise yourself with the organisation where you have gained work experience. You must document the background of the business, the staff structure as well as internal and external factors that affect the organisation. You also need to outline the following:

- The work experience job title, e.g. office assistant, trainee hairdresser, trainee programmer, trainee travel agent
- Place of work
- Branch in country/world (if applicable)
- Section (if applicable), e.g. hotel restaurant, office or bar
- Department (if applicable), e.g. sales or accounts department
- Times of work
- Name and title of superior(s)
-

Workplace Background

You should briefly describe:
- The nature of the business (service or product)
- Its history and date of establishment
- If it relocated
- Number of branches/sections/departments
- Ownership structure (sole trader, partnership, private or public limited company, state or semi-state body)
- Number of employees (including male/female breakdown)
- Size of premises

Staff Structure

You should draw one or more organisational charts showing the staff structure, emphasising clear lines of authority. The duties and responsibilities of each staff member mentioned in the chart should be described. The student examples below are taken from different vocational areas.

Visual display charts, such as bar and pie charts, can be used to depict data that applies to small, medium and large organisations. The following pie chart represents the age and gender breakdown of a company's workforce.

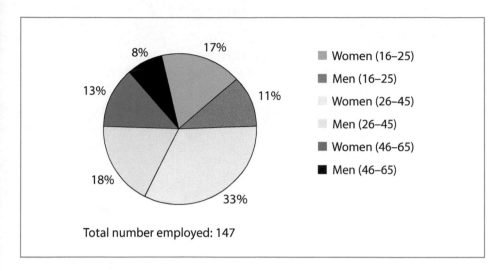

Total number employed: 147

Child Care Example

ORGANISATIONAL CHART OF A CRÈCHE

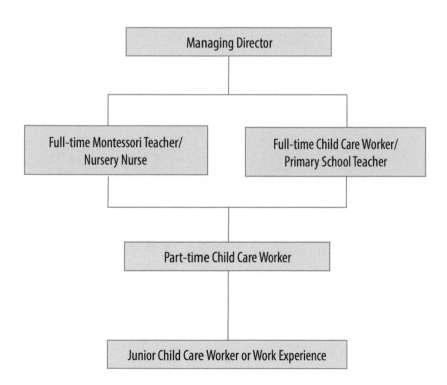

Retail Example
ORGANISATIONAL CHART OF A RETAIL OUTLET

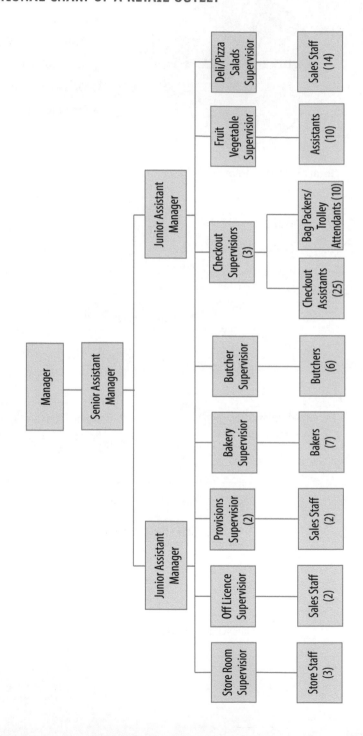

Wholesale Example

ORGANISATIONAL CHART OF A WHOLESALER

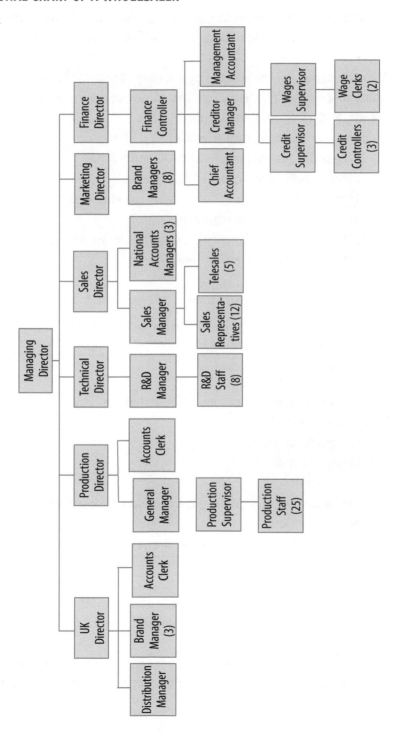

Internal Factors of the Organisation

You should also explore the internal factors that apply to your work placement and be able to explain how these factors affect the organisation.

An organisation may be affected by a variety of internal factors that dictate whether or not it is efficiently run. You could use the following questions to identify and reflect on these factors:
* Is the management style effective?
* Is the staff suitably qualified and well motivated?
* Is there a sufficient number of staff available?
* Is there an air of co-operation between members of staff?
* Is there a feeling of belonging to a team?
* Is there a problem with ongoing demands for higher wages?
* Is the equipment modern and well serviced?

Communication Methods and Professional Ethics

Good, well-defined communication methods will make for an effective, efficient organisation where everyone is fully informed and understands the workings of the organisation.

There are five channels of communication that apply to every organisation. Information travels from:
* Manager to manager
* Manager to staff
* Staff to staff
* Staff to customers, suppliers, the general public and anyone else outside the organisation
* Manager to customers, suppliers, the general public and anyone else outside the organisation

The following questions could be used to assess whether the organisation has good communication methods and whether good professional ethics are practised in the workplace:
* How do the staff and the management communicate, e.g. through meetings, notice boards, staff web zones, intercom, internal memos, etc.?

- How do staff members communicate information to customers, e.g. advertising methods, word of mouth, etc.?
- How does the manager(s) take information into and send information out of the organisation, or are other sub-managers delegated to do this work?
- What policy is in place to ensure that professional ethics are adhered to? For example, is customer confidentiality always respected? Do staff members always act professionally when dealing with customers?

Health, Hygiene and Safety in the Workplace

The following questions could be used to assess whether the organisation adheres to health, hygiene and safety guidelines:

- Does the business have a health, hygiene and safety policy? Is there a safety officer/representative on the staff?
- How does the organisation implement the policy? For example, are there appropriate exit signs? Are fire drills and precautions in place to ensure the safety of employees and the public?
- Does the business have a safety statement?
- What kind of insurance does the business have to insure itself against public liability? Are there any other types of insurance in place?
- Is there training for staff in areas such as fire prevention and first aid?
- Are there anti-bullying or anti-racist policies in place as part of the health and safety policy? What steps do the managers take to implement these?

External Factors of the Organisation

An organisation may be affected by a variety of external factors that dictate whether or not it is efficiently run. Use the following questions to identify and reflect on these factors.

- Who are the organisation's competitors?
- What kinds of market forces affect the demand, supply and prices of the goods produced or the services offered by the organisation?
- Are deliveries of supplies (incoming raw materials) or products (outgoing deliveries) often late? If so, how are sales affected?
- Have interest rate fluctuations affected the organisation in the past?
- Do currency fluctuations (exporters, importers, tourism, etc.) affect the organisation in any way?
- How do global industrial or occupational wage demands affect the organisation?

In the case of service-type organisations, the following external factors might be identified:

- Changing birth and death rates (demographics) in a region can affect a service, e.g. demand for nursing homes or child care facilities.
- Natural disasters, e.g. earthquakes, floods, volcanoes, would affect travel agents and tour operator services.
- The growth in e-commerce (buying and selling on the internet) could adversely affect those organisations not promoting their product or service on the World Wide Web.

Explore the external factors that apply to your work placement and be able to explain how these factors affect the organisation.

CHAPTER EXERCISE: WORKPLACE DETAILS
Answer the following questions in your learner's portfolio.

1. Give a brief account of the history, size, ownership and product/service profile of your workplace.
2. Draw the organisational chart of your workplace, with clear lines of authority and clear chart headings.
3. Describe the duties of the staff that are outlined in your organisational chart.
4. List the communication methods that were used in the workplace.
5. List the professional ethics that were practised by staff and managers.
6. Explain what health, safety and hygiene policy was implemented in the organisation.
7. Explain the external factors that affect your workplace.

Work Experience Diary

You should compile a detailed description of the work you undertook while on work experience.

Day-to-day experiences, both positive and negative, should be outlined. New knowledge gained and evidence of the ability to learn from negative as well as positive experiences and challenges should be shown in this report. The learner report should be based on the work experience diary.

The work experience diary should give a detailed explanation of:
* The variety of work tasks carried out while on work experience
* How work was handled
* Personal challenges encountered
* Work-related challenges encountered
* Existing skills improved upon
* New practical or interpersonal skills learned

Examples of Work Tasks

Catering	Food costing Vegetable preparation Soup making Baking Stir-fry techniques
Fashion design	Embroidery Printed textiles Advertising Fashion buying Graphic skills
Multimedia production	Digital movie processing Authoring web design Image processing Animation
Child care	Games supervision Montessori supervision Food preparation Feeding babies Changing babies

Experience Gained

You need to reflect on the practical/technical, personal and interpersonal experiences gained by undertaking various tasks. Remember:

- **Practical/technical skills** are physical work tasks, e.g. learning to use office equipment, table service duties, colouring and perming hair, graphic design techniques.
- **Personal skills** include getting to work on time, meeting deadlines, etc.
- **Interpersonal skills** are people skills, e.g. dealing courteously with the employer or supervisor, customers, service users or clients and people you work with.

The following examples explain how the tasks you are given are categorised as practical, personal and interpersonal skills.

Media/Broadcasting Student

Maeve MacDonagh, a media/broadcasting student on work experience at Live 75 FM, learned the following skills.

Practical and technical skills:

- She learned to shoot footage and edit it using Avid Xpress and Adobe Premiere Pro.
- She learned how to do vox pops and edit them using Adobe Audition.

Personal and interpersonal skills:

- Maeve learned how to be more patient when organising shoots.
- She learned to work well as part of a team.

Computer Student

Mary Ryan is on work experience in Compumarket Ltd. As part of an advertising procedure, her supervisor requested her to directly mail a variety of catalogues to potential customers. In completing this task, the experience would have taught her the following skills.

Practical and technical skills:
- She learned how to sift through customer records from a database file in order to shortlist appropriate prospective customers.
- She gained experience using the Mail Merge facility in Microsoft Word.

Personal skills:
- She learned how to work on her own initiative.
- She learned how to be more adaptable and flexible.

Interpersonal skills:
- Mary learned how to carry out supervisor instructions efficiently.
- She learned how to work efficiently with colleagues to complete the task.

Tourism Student

Colm Downey, on work experience at Going Places Travel Agency, must deal with a client from the enquiry through to the booking stage. In completing this task, the experience would have taught Colm the following skills.

Practical and technical skills:
- Colm learned how to use the computerised Galileo system efficiently. Colm was able to obtain booking information and confidently book a holiday for the client.
- He learned administration skills, including writing a receipt after the client pays (by cheque, credit card or cash) and forwarding the receipt to the client.

Personal and interpersonal skills:
- He learned how to be more punctual and improve on attendance.
- He learned how to be more competent in dealing with awkward customers.

Hairdressing Student

Siobhán McMahon, on work experience at Wedge Styles salon, learned the following skills.

Practical and technical skills:
- She learned how to wash, set and blow-dry hair.
- She learned how to apply a semi-permanent colour and a conditioning treatment.

Personal and interpersonal skills:
- Siobhán acquired a high level of tolerance working in a busy environment.
- She learned how to work effectively as part of a multi-skilled team.

Child Care Student

Eileen Daly, on work experience at Little Treasures Crèche, learned the following skills.

Practical and technical skills:
- She learned how to quickly and efficiently change babies' nappies, paying attention to hygiene.
- She learned how to assist in toilet training toddlers in co-operation with parents.
- She learned how to assist in introductory Montessori instruction.

Personal skills:
- She learned how to co-ordinate a range of children's activities, simultaneously maintaining a good degree of control.
- She learned how to strictly adhere to the time routine of the crèche for different activities, e.g. meal times, nappy changing and break times, etc.

Interpersonal skills:
- She learned how to delicately and efficiently give full comprehensive information to parents regarding their child's or children's progress using the report book for parents.

Art and Design Student

Séamus Brophy, on work experience at Graphic Design Studios, learned the following skills.

Practical and technical skills:
- He learned how to produce a book cover from designs using InDesign.
- He learned how to layer photographs using Adobe Photoshop.

Personal and interpersonal skills:
- He learned how to work on his own initiative.
- He learned how to contribute his own design ideas to a group discussion.

Challenges Encountered

You may encounter personal and work-related challenges while on work experience.

Personal challenges:
- Getting to work – good attendance
- Getting to work on time – punctuality
- Completing work tasks – ability to do the work
- Completing tasks on time – meeting deadlines

Work-related challenges:
- Dealing with awkward customers, service users or clients
- Dealing with unco-operative colleagues
- Dealing with a difficult employer/superior

Personal Challenges
- Have you become more punctual? Has your attendance improved?
- Are you being more accurate and precise in the execution of work tasks?
- Do you get tasks completed on time?
- Do you organise your work tasks in a diary in order of priority?
- Do you attend to work tasks immediately or do you still postpone them?

Work-related Challenges
Awkward customers or clients:
- Did you learn to listen and take note of the problem?
- Did you apologise for the inconvenience (even though you were not at fault) and maintain a high degree of professional courtesy?

- Did you investigate options to remedy the problem?
- Did you offer to compensate the customer or client?
- Was the problem resolved in a manner satisfactory to the customer or client?

Difficult colleagues:

- Have you learned to avoid open confrontation with colleagues?
- Do you realise the importance of not backbiting colleagues?
- Did you maintain courtesy towards colleagues at all times?
- Did you articulate your viewpoints to colleagues in a coherent and fair manner?
- Do you realise the importance of looking at the wider picture when it comes to a breakdown of relations between colleagues?

Difficult employer/superior:

- Did you learn to accept constructive criticism with dignity?
- Did you articulate your viewpoints to your employer/superior in a calm and coherent manner?
- Have you learned how to work well with a difficult employer/superior?

CHAPTER EXERCISE CHECKLIST

Make sure you have included all the exercises in this chapter in your learner's portfolio.

Chapter Exercise	Completed
Include day(s) of work experience/practice and times of work	
List and explain the tasks carried out while on work experience/practice and how they were handled – a detailed account of daily performance and learning	
An account of any work-related or personal challenges encountered	
An account of the skills you improved upon (personal, interpersonal, practical/technical)	
Visual or written evidence of participation while on work experience/practice – doing the job, e.g. photo, supervisor verification, e-mails or equivalent	

Evidence of having observed good timekeeping, e.g. clock in/out, sign in/out sheets or supervisor verification, reference e-mails or equivalent	
Evidence of having worked independently under general direction/supervision, e.g. written supervisor verification, such as reference e-mails requesting tasks to be done or equivalent	
Evidence of meeting deadlines, e.g. written supervisor verification or equivalent	
Evidence of care having been taken with personal presentation, e.g. a photo of you dressed appropriately for the work setting	
Evidence of newly learned communication skills, e.g. recordings of your new skills or evidence of new written skills, such as editing paperwork or equivalent	
Evidence of having adhered to health and safety or other relevant regulations in the workplace, e.g. signed sheet for health and safety training, equality training, fire safety training, anti-defamation training or equivalent, depending on the organisation's regulation requirements	

What Needs to Be in the Learner's Portfolio?

Learner Account of Work Placement Section
* Work experience diary with a detailed account of daily performance, learning and challenges
* Written or visual evidence of having participated in and practised employability skills while on work experience
* Evidence of having observed good timekeeping
* Evidence of having worked independently under general direction
* Evidence of having met deadlines
* Evidence of care having been taken with personal presentation
* Evidence of newly learned communication skills
* Evidence of having adhered to health and safety and other relevant regulations

CHAPTER 6

Reflecting on the Work Placement Experience

"I'm not sure you understand what I mean by career goals!"

LEARNING OUTCOMES

- PRODUCE A COMPREHENSIVE REFLECTION ON YOUR WORK EXPERIENCE.
- KEEP A DETAILED DIARY OF YOUR WORK EXPERIENCE.
- EXAMINE FEEDBACK FROM YOUR SUPERVISOR.

Upon completion of a work experience placement, you must critically analyse the learning goals achieved, the skills gained or improved upon and the experiences and challenges encountered. You are encouraged to evaluate how you would manage a similar work experience situation now – in other words, what could have been done differently?

Your mentor or supervisor will monitor your progress during the work experience placement. He or she will give you feedback on your:

- Attendance and punctuality
- Ability to work independently
- Capacity to meet deadlines
- Personal presentation
- Adherence to health and safety regulations
- Communication skills (personal, interpersonal and vocational)

Challenges

You can meet a variety of challenges during a work experience placement.

Conflict

Some examples of conflict situations that you may encounter are:
- Two fellow employees not getting along
- An employee not getting along with management
- Inadvertently doing or saying something to cause a disagreement
- Misinterpreting an instruction from your supervisor
- Making an inappropriate comment to a colleague or client

Most conflict situations can be overcome by dealing with the situation in a calm and positive manner. If an apology is necessary, it should be made quickly and sincerely.

Criticism

Your supervisor may have to offer constructive criticism during the course of your work experience placement. There are a variety of situations that may warrant constructive criticism. Some examples are:
- All of the assigned work was not completed
- The work fell below the required standard
- Punctuality and/or timekeeping was poor
- Failure to communicate with fellow employees or clients in an appropriate way
- Wearing inappropriate clothes
- Not adhering to acceptable standards of personal hygiene
- Disregarding health and safety regulations
- Isolating yourself from fellow employees

The criticism is meant to be caring and constructive. It is not helpful to react negatively to constructive criticism. You should embrace constructive criticism (within reason) and ask for clarification and guidance on the issue.

Meeting New People

Meeting new people can be stressful. Shyness can hold a person back from achieving and showing others his or her true capabilities. It is essential to believe in yourself and to show what you can offer. When communicating with a person who you are meeting for the first time, it is important to remember their name and to maintain eye contact during the conversation.

Learning in Relation to Quality Management

Quality management can be defined as guiding all the activities and tasks required to achieve excellence in the workplace. It is essential that a new employee knows what is expected of him or her in relation to the quality management of a company or organisation.

CHAPTER EXERCISE: YOUR GOALS

After you finish your work placement, examine the goals you set in Chapter 2 (pages 33–35) and then complete the following table.

	Short-term Goals	Comment
1.		

2.

3.

4.

	Medium-term Goals	Comment
1.		
2.		
3.		
4.		

	Long-term Goals	Comment
1.		
2.		
3.		
4.		

CHAPTER EXERCISE: WORK PLACEMENT DIARY

As part of the work experience assessment, you must recount your daily performance on the placement and list any new learning and challenges. You must analyse what was done each day and how it was done. The most efficient way to do this is to keep a work placement diary. You can photocopy the following template or download it from the Gill & Macmillan website (www.gillmacmillan.ie) and print as many copies as you need. Make sure your supervisor or mentor signs each sheet.

After you finish the diary, you should do a comprehensive evaluation of your own performance. Include any feedback from your mentor or supervisor. Highlight any successes and any challenges met, such as conflict, criticism, meeting new people and learning in relation to quality management. You should comment on what you could do differently in your next job.

WORK EXPERIENCE DIARY: DAY _____

Name: _____   Date: _____

Class: _____

What tasks did you undertake?

_____

_____

_____

What existing skills did you improve upon?

Personal skills: _____

Interpersonal skills: _____

Vocational skills: _____

What new skills did you learn?

_____

_____

_____

How was work handled?

_____

_____

_____

What personal or work-related challenges did you encounter?

_____

_____

_____

_____

What could you have done differently?

_____

_____

_____

Supervisor's signature: _____

CHAPTER EXERCISE CHECKLIST

Make sure you have included all the exercises in this chapter in your learner's portfolio.

Chapter Exercise	Completed
Examine the goals you set in Chapter 2 after you finish your work placement	
Fill out a work placement diary and make sure your supervisor or mentor signs each sheet, giving a summary of your personal performance while on work experience or practice	

What Needs to Be in the Learner's Portfolio?

Learner Account of the Work Placement Section
- A comprehensive reflection on the work experience, to include feedback from the supervisor or mentor on personal performance
- Evidence of experiences in the form of at least 10 workplace diary sheets, to be signed by the work experience supervisor
- Challenges revisited what could have been done differently or better

CHAPTER 7

Future Planning

"Life's too short to be in the wrong job!"

LEARNING OUTCOMES
- EXPLORE FUTURE JOB OPTIONS.
- EXPLORE POSSIBLE FUTURE EDUCATION OR TRAINING.

Work Experience and Your Future Career Plan

A career is a journey, not a destination. You must know your strengths and how to improve your skills in order to meet the challenges of the changing world of work.

A work experience placement in your chosen field will have given you clear insights into:
- The nature of the job on a daily basis
- Your suitability for this type of work
- Any knowledge gaps or skill deficits you may have
- The qualifications needed for this work

Before embarking on the world of work, you should develop a career plan. When you work on your career plan, you will likely go through the following four-step process:

1. Self-awareness
2. Narrow down your career choice
3. Make decisions
4. Take action

You should also endeavour to do a job search by checking for at least one local job, one national job and one international job connected with your vocational area.

Self-awareness

The starting point of any career plan is self-awareness. You need to do a personal SWOT analysis:

*   **S**trengths, e.g. what are your aptitudes and skills?
*   **W**eaknesses, e.g. are you a good communicator?
*   **O**pportunities, e.g. where are the job openings?
*   **T**hreats, e.g. are many people competing for jobs in the career that you are interested in?

The work experience portfolio that you have already compiled during your recent work placement will be an excellent aid in producing your personal SWOT analysis.

CHAPTER EXERCISE: SWOT ANALYSIS

Update your personal career SWOT analysis from Chapter 1 (page 12) using this table.

PERSONAL CAREER SWOT ANALYSIS	
Strengths	1.
	2.
	3.

Weaknesses	1.
	2.
	3.
Opportunities	1.
	2.
	3.
Threats	1.
	2.
	3.

Narrow Down Your Career Choice

You need to research careers that interest you and their respective educational or training requirements. Once you have some idea of your job preferences, you can look at the specific skills and qualifications needed for those occupations.

* How do your skills and interests match up with the occupations that interest you?
* What type of work is available and where is it located (online and address)?

Here are some useful websites to help you narrow down your career options:
* www.careersportal.ie
* www.recruitireland.com
* http://careersireland.wordpress.com

Make Decisions

You need to narrow down your career options and think about what career suits you best. Ask yourself the following questions:
* What are my best work options? Why?
* How do they match up with my skills, interests and values?
* How do they fit with the current labour market?
* How do they sit with my current situation and responsibilities?
* What are my options for acquiring the knowledge or skills?
* Do I need full-time or part-time education and/or a training course?
* What qualification will I receive on completing the course?
* Where does the qualification sit in the National Framework of Qualifications (NFQ) and the European Qualifications Framework (EQF)?

- What are my options for earning further qualifications? (For example, will a particular FETAC/QQI Level 5 or 6 certificate allow you to progress to degree programmes in this area at an IT or university?)
- Can I support myself financially during a period of formal education/ training?

National Framework of Qualifications (NFQ)

'The National Framework of Qualifications (NFQ) provides a way to compare qualifications and to ensure that they are quality assured and recognised at home and abroad' (www.nfq.ie).

European Qualifications Framework (EQF)

'The European Qualifications Framework (EQF) for lifelong learning provides a common reference framework that helps to compare the national qualifications systems, frameworks and their levels. It makes qualifications more readable and understandable across different countries and systems in Europe and thus promotes lifelong and life-wide learning and the mobility of European citizens, whether for studying or working abroad' (http://ec.europa.eu/).

Take Action

This is where you plan the steps you need to take to put your plan into action. Use everything you have learned about your skills, interests and values together with the information you have gathered about the world of work to create your plan.

Start by asking yourself the following questions:
- What actions or steps will help me achieve my work, training and career goals?
- Where can I get help?
- Who will support me?

CHAPTER EXERCISE: YOUR CAREER PLAN

Using your completed work experience portfolio and the answers to the questions posed in the previous sections, complete the following table.

MY CAREER PLAN	
What are my best personal qualities?	
What skills and educational qualifications do I have?	
What careers would best suit me?	
What specific skills and knowledge do I still need to make me employable in my number one choice career?	
How am I going to master these skills and get this knowledge?	
If I need a formal qualification to be eligible for a job in my chosen career, how and where am I going to get it?	
How long will my course or training take?	

What is the job market like in my chosen career area in Ireland right now?	
What is the job market like in my chosen career area abroad right now?	

CHAPTER EXERCISE: SEARCH FOR JOB VACANCIES

Search online for job vacancies in your areas of interest. Your research should include one local, one national and one international job advert in your chosen vocational area. This will give you a good idea of where jobs exist. It might influence your decision to remain in Ireland or to travel abroad in search of future work.

Local job advert	
National job advert	
International job advert	

Further Education Opportunities

The best place to search for up-to-date information on how to progress from FETAC/QQI courses to higher education diploma and degree courses is on the Central Applications Office (CAO) website (www.cao.ie). Meet with your guidance counsellor to assess the best options for you regarding further or higher education or transferring to courses.

How can I use my FETAC/QQI award to progress to third level?

Many learners complete post-Leaving Certificate or further education and training courses leading to FETAC/QQI Level 5 or 6 awards with the specific intention of using their award to progress to third level through a system known as the Higher Education Links Scheme. This scheme has been in existence for over a decade.

Applicants must submit their third-level applications to the CAO by 1 February in the year in which they are applying. Detailed information is available on www.cao.ie. In July, FETAC/QQI results are issued to the CAO. Details of how applicants are assessed vary somewhat between third-level institutions, but all information can be found on www.cao.ie. A new scoring system for your FETAC/QQI awards applies from 2013.

Please note – universities and some higher education institutions offer places from a reserved quota. In general, institutes of technology offer places from a list ranking FETAC/QQI achievements with other candidates who apply based on Leaving Certificate.

What is the certification cost?

These costs can be checked by visiting the FETAC/QQI website.

Does FETAC/QQI offer grants to learners?

FETAC/QQI does not provide funding for individual learners or courses. We would suggest you contact the Department of Education directly and also your local County/City Council and ask to speak to someone in the Education Grants section. In addition, information on financial support for further and higher education is available at www.studentfinance.ie or Student Universal Support Ireland (www.susi.ie).

Note: Check the FETAC/QQI website for more information on certification fees and rules. To see if you might be eligible for maintenance grants, check the information at www.studentfinance.ie.

CHAPTER EXERCISE CHECKLIST

Make sure you have included all the exercises in this chapter in your learner's portfolio.

Chapter Exercise	Completed
Update your personal career SWOT analysis from Chapter 1	
Create your career plan	
Search for job vacancies	

What Needs to Be in the Learner's Portfolio?

Planning and Preparation Section
- Link experience from your work placement to your future career or work plan
- Explore options for future education and training
- Explore future options of employment

CHAPTER 8

Skills Demonstration: Supervisor Reports

"We should probably take one of those down."

LEARNER OUTCOMES

- OBSERVE GOOD TIMEKEEPING.
- WORK INDEPENDENTLY WHILE UNDER GENERAL DIRECTION.
- MEET DEADLINES.
- TAKE CARE WITH YOUR PERSONAL PRESENTATION.
- FOLLOW HEALTH, SAFETY AND OTHER RELEVANT REGULATIONS.
- DEMONSTRATE GOOD COMMUNICATION SKILLS IN THE WORKPLACE (PERSONAL, INTERPERSONAL AND VOCATIONAL).

The Supervisor's Report

The supervisor's report is an important part of the overall assessment of your FETAC/QQI Work Experience module. It assesses a broad range of vocational, practical and interpersonal communication skills you demonstrated in the workplace.

Areas that the supervisor must assess are:
- Observation of good timekeeping – punctuality and attendance
- Meeting deadlines
- Personal presentation
- Adherence to health and safety and other relevant regulations
- Demonstrate effective personal communication skills
- Demonstrate effective interpersonal communication skills
- Demonstrate effective technological communication skills
- Working independently while under general direction (Level 5 – see guidelines in this chapter)
- Working independently according to prior planning (Level 6 only – see guidelines in this chapter)

Sample Supervisor's Report FETAC/QQI Level 5

The following blank FETAC/QQI Level 5 report form (reproduced from the FETAC/QQI Work Experience module) is given to the supervisor.

Level 5 Work Experience 5N1356 - Supervisor's Report

Learners Name: _____ Centre/School Name: _____ Tel No: _____

Organisation/Company Name: _____ Supervisor's Name: _____ No of days worked: _____

Guidelines: This report forms an important part of the overall assessment of Level 5 Work Experience 5N1356 for FETAC certification. It should be completed by a supervisor/manager who has observed the Learner in the workplace. The Workplace Supervisor/Manager should indicate the Learner's performance by placing a tick for each of the criteria under one of the headings. *Excellent should only be used in cases of outstanding performance*

Criteria	Excellent	Very Good	Good	Satisfactory	Unsatisfactory	Unable to Assess	Supervisor/Assessor Comments
Observation of good timekeeping							Brief description of work undertaken by Learner
Working independently while under general direction							
Meeting deadlines							Any comments or suggestions on work experience arrangements
Personal presentation							
Adherence to health, safety and other relevant regulations							
Demonstrate effective personal communication skills							
Demonstrate effective interpersonal communication skills							Any other comments
Demonstrate effective technological communication skills							

Learner Signature: _____ Date: _____

Signature of Workplace Supervisor: _____ Date: _____

Signature of Assessor: _____ Date: _____

FOR FETAC/QQI WORK EXPERIENCE LEVEL 5

Work Experience 5N1356	Learner Marking Sheet Skills Demonstration 40%

Learner's Name: _____   Learner's PPSN: _____

Assessment Criteria	Maximum Mark	Learner Mark
Work Experience Supervisor's Report	40	
Satisfactory in at least 6 categories: 15 -23 marks		
Good in all categories or *very good* in at least 6 categories: 24 - 31 marks		
Very good in all categories or *excellent* in at least 6 categories: 32-40 marks		
TOTAL MARKS	40	

Assessor's Signature: _____   Date: _____

External Authenticator's Signature: _____   Date: _____

Forty per cent of all the marks for the FETAC/QQI Work Experience module are set aside for the supervisor's report form. In grading the form, the examiner awards marks based on the supervisor's entries, as follows:

- Satisfactory in **at least six** categories (15–23 marks)
- Good in **all** categories **or** very good in **at least six** categories (24–31 marks)
- Very good in **all** categories or excellent in **at least six** categories (32–40 marks)

Note: In the work practice mode, where the teacher/tutor/co-ordinator elects to monitor and assess the learner, the teacher/tutor completes the report form.

Sample Supervisor's Report FETAC/QQI Level 6

The following blank FETAC/QQI Level 6 report form (reproduced from the FETAC/QQI Work Experience module) is given to the supervisor.

Level 6 Work Experience 6N1946
Employers Report

Learners Name: _____   Centre/School Name: _____   Tel No: _____

Organisation/Company Name: _____   Supervisor's Name: _____   No of days worked: _____

Guidelines: This report forms an important part of the overall assessment of Level 6 Work Experience 6N1946 for FETAC certification. It should be completed by a supervisor/manager who has observed the Learner in the workplace. The Workplace Supervisor/Manager should indicate the Learner's performance by placing a tick for each of the criteria under one of the headings. Excellent should only be used in cases of outstanding performance.

Criteria	Excellent	Very Good	Good	Satisfactory	Unsatisfactory	Unable to Assess	Supervisor's Comments
Punctuality and attendance							
Initiative							
Working independently according to prior planning							
Meeting deadlines in the implementation and evaluation of task							
Demonstration of good practice							
Understanding of health and safety-issues and other relevant regulations							
Demonstrate effective personal communication skills with staff/clients							
Demonstrate effective interpersonal communication skills throughout the task							
Demonstrate effective technological communication skills as required							
Acceptance of direction/criticism							

Learner Signature: _____ | Date: _____

Signature of Workplace Supervisor: _____   Date: _____

Signature of Assessor: _____   Date: _____

FOR FETAC/QQI WORK EXPERIENCE LEVEL 6

Work Experience 6N1946	Learner Marking Sheet Skills Demonstration 40%		

Learner's Name: _____   Learner's PPSN: _____

Assessment Criteria	Maximum Mark	Learner Mark
Work Experience Employer Report	40	
Satisfactory in at least 8 categories: 15 – 23 marks *Good* in all categories or *very good* in at least 8 categories: 23 – 31 marks *Very good* in all categories or *excellent* in at least 8 categories: 32 – 40 marks		
Total Mark	40	

Assessor's Signature: _____   Date: _____

External Authenticator's Signature: _____   Date: _____

Forty per cent of all the marks for the FETAC/QQI Work Experience module are set aside for the supervisor's report form. In grading the form, the examiner awards marks based on the supervisor's entries, as follows:

- Satisfactory in **at least eight** categories (15–23 marks)
- Good in **all** categories **or** very good in **at least eight** categories (24–31 marks)
- Very good in **all** categories or excellent in **at least eight** categories (32–40 marks)

Guidelines for the Supervisor

The supervisor must complete the form as accurately and as objectively as possible in order to give a measured indication of your abilities and application. In completing the form, the supervisor gives a brief description of the work you carried out and is encouraged to comment on what he or she believes are more suitable arrangements for work experience to be conducted, based on the particular vocational area their organisation is connected to. The supervisor should maintain regular contact with the course provider to ensure best-quality learner work, for the benefit of both the organisation and the work experience participant. This will lead to enhanced learner performance in the workplace. It is also a positive way of addressing any skills shortages that may be apparent.

Guidelines for the Learner

While on work experience, you will be assessed in the following areas.

Good Timekeeping

- **Punctuality:** Consistent late arrival for work is frowned upon in most organisations. If you are going to be late for work for an unforeseen reason, call the supervisor and let them know when you will arrive.
- **Attendance at workplace:** Inconsistent attendance at work leads to dismissal in most organisations. If you can't go to work, call the supervisor and tell him or her the reason for your absence.

Meet Deadlines and Quality of Work

Poorly carried out or incomplete work or work that is not completed on time does not reflect well on you. If you feel that the supervisor is unhappy with your work, ask for guidance on how the work could have been carried out better. If more time was needed to get it done, you need to discuss this and request it.

Personal Presentation

While some organisations may enforce a strict dress code, nowadays most accept neat, casual dress in the workplace. Runners, dirty and/or torn jeans are not recommended. Heavy make-up and wearing too much scent are generally frowned upon. A little common sense is required when dressing for the workplace and an excellent level of personal hygiene is the norm for organisations' employees in order to promote a good company image.

Follow Health and Safety and Other Relevant Regulations

You must make yourself aware of the health and safety procedures within the organisation. A quiet conversation with your supervisor on this topic before starting your work experience is recommended.

Demonstrate Effective Personal Communication Skills

- **Reliable, loyal, hardworking:** It is essential to adopt a hardworking approach to work and work experience and to be reliable regarding what you say you will do and time management. Learners should show loyalty and act in a professional manner. This is part and parcel of the professional work ethic expected of workers.

- **Interest in the work:** A lack of enthusiasm or a general lackadaisical attitude to work becomes apparent to a supervisor very quickly. An eagerness to undertake and carry out work with a positive, cheerful disposition is required.
- **Acceptance of direction or criticism:** You can expect some constructive direction or criticism from your supervisor, which will be given to help you become a more effective worker. Do not develop a defensive approach to the supervisor's guidance. Listen carefully and be prepared to ask further questions to clarify the points being made to you.
- **Ability to follow instructions:** Listening is an essential part of communication. If you are given a set of instructions at the start of the day, it is good practice to make a note of each one in the order that they were given. If you get an instruction that you do not understand, always ask for clarification before starting the task. By simply repeating a question, you can gain the required clarification from the supervisor.
- **Initiative:** Initiative is described as 'the power or ability to begin or to follow through energetically with a plan or task without prompting or direction from others'. It implies enterprise and determination. It is a positive attribute, but as a new worker you must be careful not to undertake a radical course of action without first discussing the idea with a supervisor.
- **Adaptability:** The ability to adjust your approach and be flexible in changing and challenging situations is another quality that is very useful in the workplace.

Demonstrate Effective Interpersonal Communication Skills

- **Relating to co-workers:** After the initial introductory period, most workers settle in as part of an effective work team. An ability to work alongside colleagues to complete tasks is essential in most organisations.
- **Relating to supervisor:** While on work experience, you must listen carefully to your supervisor's instructions and carry them out to the best of your ability.
- **Communicating with customers:** 'The customer is always right' is a good motto to adopt when dealing with members of the general public. Without

customers, the business will quickly fail. You can occasionally be confronted with difficult customers who wish to vent their spleen. In such situations, remain calm and do not engage in an argument. Call the supervisor if you feel that you may not be able to deal with the customer's queries or complaints.

Demonstrate Effective Technological Communication Skills

When you learn a skill, two steps are required:
- Observe the skill being carried out by an expert practitioner
- Frequently repeat the skill to fully master it

Whether you are observing a hair stylist applying a hair colour or a computer technician installing a hard disk, the ease with which the expert carries out the skill should be noted.

The prudent use and care of workplace equipment is also important. For example, a painter does not leave his paintbrushes strewn on the floor at the end of the day, a network engineer does not use work time to download music albums for her iPod and a forklift operator does not stack pallets too high.

Working Independently While Under General Direction (Level 5)

The ability to work on your own under supervision is important while being given general direction by a supervisor.

Working Independently According to Prior Planning (Level 6)

At Level 6 (under the section 'Working independently according to prior planning'), you will be assessed on your ability to demonstrate supervisory skills and capacities, to include the skills and qualities required for a particular post in the public, private or voluntary sector.

You must take on a specific task with permission from the supervisor and manage this task yourself. In doing so, you will demonstrate and showcase your supervisory or management skills.

Specifically, you must demonstrate how to effectively participate and practise employability skills while on work experience, to include the following.

- Observing good timekeeping
    - Attendance and punctuality
    - Agreed timescale to carry out a specific task or activity, including prior permission given from supervisor
- Working independently on an agreed specific task or activity
- Personal presentation to undertake task or activity
    - Appropriate dress
    - Attention to personal hygiene
- Organisational skills
    - Equipment or materials available prior to start of task or activity
    - Correct environment to carry out task or activity
- Communication
    - Agreed time and place from supervisor to carry out task or activity
    - Clarifying instructions to the individual or group before carrying out the task or activity
    - Formal/informal communication during the task/activity
- Following health, safety and other relevant regulations
    - Responsibilities under the regulations
    - Relevant employment regulations
    - Reporting procedures
- Meeting deadlines relative to the specific task or activity
    - Tasks completed according to plan
    - Confirm completion of the task or activity with supervisor

The level of independent self-directed learning required at Level 6 is emphasised. Level 6 learners are expected to work independently according to prior planning and showcase their supervisory and employability skills by means of self-direction and by displaying good judgement with regard to all aspects of the task that they lead, including efficient supervisory or management skills.

Level 5 learners are expected to work independently but under general direction. Therefore, Level 5 learners are more reliant on the supervisor's direction.

The following table lists examples of possible tasks at Level 6 in different vocational areas.

Mode	Examples of Possible Tasks
Under the work practice mode	• Leading a student team to produce a radio programme for a student radio station • Leading a student team to run an event
Under the work experience mode	• Be in charge of a promotional campaign that involves other members of staff – agree plans with the supervisor, manage the job and show results in the form of increased sales or otherwise • Be in charge of devising a new and improved customer charter or customer service policy with a team of staff members • Be responsible for reviewing the methods used in a childcare workplace or setting to devise a new and improved health and safety policy that is in line with health board quality assurance guidelines • Lead an art team to enhance the visual impression of an organisation

CHAPTER EXERCISE: SKILLS DEMONSTRATION

1. Write a brief account of the main points on the supervisor's form that you should pay attention to while on work experience.
2. Note particular areas of assessment that you need to pay attention to while on work experience.

CHAPTER EXERCISE CHECKLIST

Make sure you have included all the exercises in this chapter in your learner's portfolio.

Chapter Exercise	Completed
Write a brief account of the main points on the supervisor's form that you should pay attention to while on work experience	
Note particular areas of assessment that you need to pay attention to while on work experience	

What Needs to Be in the Learner's Portfolio?

Skills Demonstration Section
*   The appropriate supervisor's report

CHAPTER 9

Work Practice

"Apples are fine, but I find today's
teacher prefers a nice latte."

LEARNING OUTCOMES

- SUMMARISE THE DISTINGUISHING FEATURES OF THE ORGANISATION, INSTITUTION OR WORKPLACE.
- COMMENT ON CURRENT ISSUES, CHALLENGES AND TRENDS AFFECTING THE ORGANISATION, INSTITUTION OR WORKPLACE.
- SUMMARISE THE MAIN LEGISLATION AND REGULATIONS RELEVANT TO THE WORKPLACE.
- EXPLAIN THE ORGANISATION'S INTERNAL AND EXTERNAL POLICIES AND PROCEDURES THAT ARE PERTINENT TO YOUR OWN ROLE AND THE ROLE OF OTHERS.
- CONCLUDE A MINIMUM TWO-MONTH WORK PRACTICE OR PLACEMENT, UNDERTAKING A RANGE OF VOCATIONALLY SPECIFIC TASKS AND ACTIVITIES.
- SELECT INFORMATION REQUIRED FOR A RANGE OF WORK-BASED TASKS.
- WORK INDEPENDENTLY, CARRYING OUT A RANGE OF VOCATIONALLY SPECIFIC ACTIVITIES AND TASKS IN THE ORGANISATION, INSTITUTION OR WORKPLACE, SEEKING ADVICE AND GENERAL DIRECTION AS APPROPRIATE.
- DEMONSTRATE MEMBERSHIP OF THE TRAINING ORGANISATION OR TEAM.
- MAINTAIN TIMEKEEPING, TAKE CARE WITH YOUR PERSONAL PRESENTATION, MEET DEADLINES AND FOLLOW HEALTH AND SAFETY AND OTHER RELEVANT REGULATIONS AND PRACTICE.

- EXECUTE WORK PRACTICE TASKS AND RESPONSIBILITIES IN A PROFESSIONAL AND SAFE MANNER.
- REFLECT ON YOUR PERSONAL WORK PRACTICES, TO INCLUDE FEEDBACK FROM YOUR SUPERVISOR(S) OR MENTOR(S) ON PERSONAL PERFORMANCE, ACHIEVEMENTS AND CHALLENGES.
- REVIEW YOUR PERSONAL AND PROFESSIONAL LEARNING.

Work practice involves undertaking **simulated or real work** within your own college or centre's environment, where work is monitored by the tutor, teacher or co-ordinator.

How to Put the Portfolio of Work Together

The following is a guide to successfully compiling your portfolio. Use these headings to organise your work-related evidence and refer to the appropriate chapters in this book (see the checklist on page 139).

Collection of Work (40%)

Part 1: Evidence of Analysing the Features of an Organisation or Institution

Your work-related evidence should include:

- A summary of challenges, trends and current issues at local, national and global level.
- Include a consideration of social, economic and ethical issues.
- Describe the organisation's internal and external policies and procedures that are pertinent to your own role and to the role of others.

Tips to achieve the above work-related evidence:

- Research work organisations, e.g. types (public, private, voluntary sector), structures and roles, including:
  - ◆ Size, organisational structure, main aims and the overall work
  - ◆ Staff–client engagement
  - ◆ Management practices

- Study current work-related issues, e.g. challenges and trends, including:
    - ◆ Local demographic change
    - ◆ National immigration or emigration
    - ◆ Global new technologies
    - ◆ Economic trends
    - ◆ Social and ethical criteria, e.g. education level for potential employees

Part 2: A Synopsis of the Rights and Responsibilities of Employees and Employers

Your work-related evidence should include:
- Health, safety and welfare at work, e.g. by referring to relevant legislation
- Equality legislation, e.g. rights with regard to the nine grounds of discrimination as referenced in the equality legislation
- Union representation
- Regulations relating to pay, e.g. minimum wage, annual leave, maternity leave, parental leave

Tips to achieve the above work-related evidence:
- You need to summarise the basic rights and responsibilities of employees and employers in the particular work, organisational or institutional context of the vocational area of the programme, to include each of the points above.

Part 3: A Reflection on Your Personal Work Practice

Your work-related evidence should include:
- Feedback from your supervisor(s) or mentor(s) on your personal performance, achievements and challenges, such as teamwork, appreciation of diverse work ethics, meeting new people and learning in relation to various forms of quality management.

Tips to achieve the above work-related evidence:
- Research the organisation's internal and external policies and procedures in relation to your own role and the role of others.
- Check the appropriate chapters of this book to help you compile Part 1, Part 2 and Part 3 of the evidence needed.

Learner's Record (60%)

Your learner record must include:

- A completed work experience employer report (see the sample report in this chapter)
- An account of your work practice (i.e. your daily performance, learning and challenges), including:
    - ◆ Feedback from your supervisor(s) or mentor(s) on your personal performance
    - ◆ Challenges such as conflict, criticism, meeting new people and learning in relation to quality management
- A comprehensive evaluation of your work practice or placement, including:
    - ◆ Learning outcomes achieved
    - ◆ Opportunities for further education or training
    - ◆ Analysis of key challenges

Tips to achieve the above learner's record evidence:

- Conclude a minimum two-month work practice placement, undertaking a range of vocationally specific tasks and activities.
- Select information required for a range of work-based tasks, to include analysis of information and application of knowledge to new situations.
- Work independently, carrying out a range of vocationally specific activities and tasks in the organisation, institution or workplace, seeking advice and general direction as appropriate.
- Contribute positively as a member of an organisation or team. Maintain timekeeping, take care with your personal presentation, meet deadlines and follow health and safety and other relevant regulations and practice.
- Execute work practice tasks and responsibilities in a professional and safe manner. Produce documentary evidence of achieved tasks using worksheets or a work diary.
- Review your personal and professional learning, including identifying your own strengths and weaknesses, learning and career opportunities within the vocational field and within the organisation, institution or workplace.

Checklist

	Did you check the matching chapter in this book to make sure you have enough detailed content in your portfolio?	Tick when the section is completed and list the date
Collection of work (40%)		
Part 1: Evidence of analysing the features of an organisation or institution	Chapter 1 Chapter 3 See also Chapter 2 (for personal challenges)	
Part 2: A synopsis of the rights and responsibilities of employees and employers	Chapter 4	
Part 3: A reflection on your personal work practice	Chapter 6 Chapter 7	
Learner record (60%)		
A completed work experience employer report	Chapter 8	
An account of your work practice	Chapter 5	
A comprehensive evaluation of your work practice or placement	Chapter 6 See also the challenges listed in Chapters 2 and 3	

You can present evidence for this assessment technique in the form of written, oral, graphic, audio and visual or any combination of these. Any audio, video or digital evidence must be provided in a suitable format. The teacher, tutor or co-ordinator must conduct random checks to ensure reliability of evidence.

Sample Mark Sheet (Collection of Work)

Work Practice 5N1433	Learner Marking Sheet Portfolio/Collection of Work 40%

Learner's Name: _____ Learner's PPSN: _____

Assessment Criteria	Maximum Mark	Mark
Work Related evidence to include	15	
• Evidence of analysing the features of an organisation/institution		
○ A summary of challenges, trends, current issues at local, national, and global level.		
○ To include consideration of social, economic and ethical issues.		
○ Describe the organisation's internal and external policies and procedures pertinent to own role and role of others		
A synopsis of rights and responsibilities of employees and employers to include	10	
○ Health, safety and welfare at work, for example by referring to relevant legislation		
○ Equality legislation, for example rights with regard to the nine grounds as referenced in the equality legislation		
○ Union representation		
○ Regulations relating to pay, for example minimum wage, annual leave, maternity leave, parental leave		
A reflection on personal work practices to include	15	
○ feedback from supervisor(s) or mentors on personal performance, achievements and challenges such as teamwork, appreciation of diverse work ethics, meeting new people and learning in relation to various forms of quality management.		
Total Marks	40	

Assessor's Signature: _____ Date: _____

Work Practice 5N1433	Learner Marking Sheet Learner Record 60%

Learner's Name: _____ Learner's PPSN: _____

Assessment Criteria	Maximum Mark	Mark
Work Practice: Employer report	20	
Satisfactory in at least 6 categories: 5– 10 marks		
Good in all categories or very good in at least 6 categories: 11 – 16 marks		
Very good in all categories or excellent in at least 6 categories: 17 – 20 marks		
Account of Work Practice	20	
○ an account of daily performance, learning and challenges		
○ a comprehensive reflection on their work experience to include		
○ feedback from supervisor or mentor on personal performance		
○ challenges such as conflict, criticism, meeting new people and learning in relation to quality management		
A comprehensive evaluation on their Work Practice to include	20	
○ learning outcomes achieved		
○ opportunities for further education/training		
○ analysing key challenges for		
Total Marks	60	

Assessor's Signature: _____ Date: _____

External Authenticator's Signature: _____ Date: _____

Sample Employer/Supervisor Report

See Chapter 8 for general guidelines on the criteria listed in the employer/ supervisor report.

Level 5 Work Practice 5N1433 - Employers Report

Learner's Name: _____ Centre/School Name: _____ Tel No.: _____

Organisation/ Company Name: _____ Supervisor's Name: _____ No of Days worked: _____

Guidelines: This report forms an important part of the overall assessment of Level 5 Work Practice 5N1433 for FETAC certification. It should be completed by a Supervisor/Manager who has observed the Learner in the workplace. The Workplace Supervisor/Manager should indicate the Learner's performance by placing a tick for each of the criteria under one of the headings. *Excellent should only be used in cases of outstanding performance*

Criteria	Excellent	Very Good	Good	Satisfactory	Unsatisfactory	Unable To Access	Supervisor/Assessors Comments
Observation of good timekeeping / Attendance							Brief Description of Work Practice undertaken
Working autonomously while under general direction							
Meeting deadlines							
Task completion / verification							Any Comments or Suggestions on task and individual performance
Adherence to health, safety and other relevant regulations							
Demonstrate effective personal / technological communication skills							Any other comments

Signature of Learner _____ Date_____

Signature of Workplace Supervisor_____ Date_____

Signature of Internal Assessor _____ Date_____

What Needs to Be in the Learner's Portfolio?

1. Collection of Work (40%)
- Evidence of analysing the features of an organisation or institution
- A synopsis of the rights and responsibilities of employees and employers
- A reflection on your personal work practice

2. Learner Record (60%)
- A completed work experience employer report
- An account of your work practice
- A comprehensive evaluation of your work practice or placement

CHAPTER 10

FETAC/QQI Level 6 Work Experience

"I'm thinking of transferring to another school of thought..."

LEARNING OUTCOMES

- PARTICIPATE IN A PLACEMENT AND DEMONSTRATE YOUR ABILITY TO WORK AT A LEVEL OF HIGHER CRAFT, JUNIOR TECHNICIAN OR SUPERVISORY ROLE.
- ANALYSE THE WORLD OF WORK AND EMPLOYMENT.
- PLAN AND PREPARE FOR SUCCESSFUL PARTICIPATION IN A RELEVANT WORK PLACEMENT.
- REFLECT ON PREPARATION FOR, UNDERTAKING AND COMPLETION OF YOUR WORK EXPERIENCE.
- DEVELOP AN UNDERSTANDING OF THE UP-TO-DATE THEORETICAL AND/OR TECHNICAL KNOWLEDGE UNDERPINNING PRACTICE IN A PARTICULAR AREA OF WORK.

- TAKE RESPONSIBILITY FOR YOUR OWN LEARNING AND DEMONSTRATE SUPERVISORY SKILLS.
- REFLECT ON CHALLENGES AND OPPORTUNITIES IN THE CHOSEN VOCATIONAL AREA.
- EVALUATE YOUR WORK PLACEMENT EXPERIENCE BASED ON FEEDBACK FROM YOUR SUPERVISOR AND ITS IMPACT ON YOUR PERSONAL CAREER CHOICE.

Level 6 is a more advanced level of learning that involves more critical thinking and analysis than is required at Level 5. The aim of Level 6 Work Experience is to provide you with:
- A comprehensive range of skills
- A detailed theoretical understanding of the general supervisory nature of the work placement in a specific vocational area

The course consists of 150 hours of typical learner effort and includes both directed and self-directed learning. The programme can be delivered through classroom-based learning activities, group discussions, one-to-one tutorials, field trips, case studies, role plays and other suitable activities as appropriate.

A minimum of 20 days or 120 hours of work experience placement must be completed in an established organisation that has been deemed suitable to provide appropriate work experience. This work placement must be appropriate to the vocational area. The work experience can be paid or voluntary. It can take place in the private, community or public sector. Some vocational areas will require additional work experience time – refer to the relevant programme descriptor for specific information regarding work experience requirements.

How to Put the Portfolio of Work Together

The following is a guide to successfully compiling your portfolio, which is worth 60%. Use these headings to organise your work and refer to the appropriate chapters in this book.

Planning and Preparation (20% of Marks)

Work Organisations

Provide evidence of extensive research on a variety of work organisations (evidence of job search skills/internet search, such as e-mails exchanged, letters sent or received), to identify one specific workplace relevant to personal career opportunities.

Work-related Issues, Trends and Needs

Provide evidence of extensive research on personal career opportunities in your chosen vocational area (public, private or voluntary area of work).

- Show an understanding of work-related issues, trends and needs: working hours, flexible/shift work, pay, safety, job stress, challenges, dress code, career progression.
- Demonstrate knowledge of the up-to-date theoretical and/or technical knowledge underpinning a particular area of work.
- Explore and understand concepts and terms related to work, such as the changing nature of work, employment/unemployment, communication and employability skills needed in the current work environment relevant to the chosen vocational area, globalisation and career management.
-

Skills Audit

This is a comprehensive personal and vocational skills audit (personal, interpersonal and practical skills you have, hope to improve on or new ones you hope to learn on work experience). Information must be relevant to the chosen vocational area and must include evidence of *prior* knowledge and learning.

CV, Letter of Application for Work Experience and Personal Statement

Include the following three documents:

- Letter of application for work experience
- Curriculum vitae
- Personal statement (with reference to qualifications)

Career Plan

A comprehensive career plan for your vocational area must include:

- Statement of learning goals (identify education and training needs)
- Action points for these goals and for the overall work experience (developments, opportunities and career paths)

Work Placement Plans

This is a statement of contractual arrangements concerning the work placement.

- Task: A detailed plan for a specific task or activity to be carried out while in work placement, including permission from your supervisor.

Vocational Study (10% of Marks)

Challenges in the Vocational Area – Locally, Nationally and Globally

This is an analysis of the key challenges and opportunities facing a particular specialised vocational area (locally, nationally and globally), including a reflection on the impact of these on your personal career choice and direction.

- Show evidence of having analysed effective participation and practice skills relevant to your chosen area.

The Rights and Responsibilities of Employees and Employers

This is an analysis of the rights and responsibilities of employees and employers in your particular specialised area of work in an organisational or institutional context, including:

- Health, safety and welfare at work
- Equality legislation
- Union representation
- Regulations related to pay and confidentiality

Your analysis should also include the following:

- Show evidence of your organisational skills with reference to health and safety, etc., such as how to keep yourself safe and informed about work-related regulations based on legislation.
- Show evidence of communication skills with your supervisor concerning the chosen task or activity to be completed.
- Show evidence of meeting deadlines connected with a specific task or activity arranged with your supervisor.

Learner Account of Work Placement (20% of Marks)
Learner Account of Work Placement
This is a detailed account of your daily performance, learning and challenges.
* Show evidence of your ability to take responsibility for your own learning.
* Show evidence of having demonstrated supervisory skills and capacities, including the skills and qualities required for a particular post in the public, private or voluntary sector.

Reflection on and Critical Analysis of Your Work Experience
This is a critical analysis and reflection on your work experience, to include:
* Positive and negative aspects of the work experience
* Overall conclusion regarding your future career options

Evaluate your work placement experience based on feedback from your supervisor and its impact on your personal career choice.

Future Planning (10% of Marks)
* Show evidence of having researched future education and training in light of your work experience.
* Show evidence of having researched employment options in light of work experience, including evidence of having explored the possibility of setting up your own business.

Checklist

	Did you check the matching chapter in this book to make sure you have enough detailed content in your portfolio?	Tick when the section is completed and list the date
Planning and preparation (20%)		
Work organisations	Chapter 1	
Work-related trends, issues and needs	Chapter 1	
Skills audit	Chapter 2	
CV, letter of application for work experience and personal statement	Chapter 2	

Career plan	Chapters 1 and 7	
Work placement plans	Chapters 1, 2, 3 and 4	
Vocational study (10%)		
Challenges in the vocational area – locally, nationally, globally	Chapter 1	
The rights and responsibilities of employees and employers	Chapter 4	
Learner account of work placement (20%)		
Learner account of work placement	Chapter 5 (see also the work experience diary sheets with feedback section in Chapter 6)	
Reflection on and critical analysis of your work experience	Chapter 6	
Future planning (10%)		
Future planning	Chapter 7	

Research Outline and Timeline: What to Do and When to Do It

For Level 6 Work Experience, you need to plan and time your activities, as many of the work activities are self-directed and based on your own initiative. Use the table below to help you.

Date	What I plan to do today	Timeline: How long I am giving myself to do it	Type of research or portfolio work I plan to do	Reminders

What Needs to Be in the Learner's Portfolio?

Work Experience FETAC/QQI Level 6

Everything that is in the above list is needed to satisfy the requirements for the Level 6 Work Experience portfolio. Follow the headings exactly and tick them off in the checklist on pages 146–147 when you have completed them.

1. Portfolio of Work (60%)

- Planning and Preparation (20%)
- Vocational Study (10%)
- Learner Account of Work Placement (20%)
- Future Planning (10%)

2. Work Experience Employer/Supervisor Report (40%)